100 YEARS
100 BUILDINGS

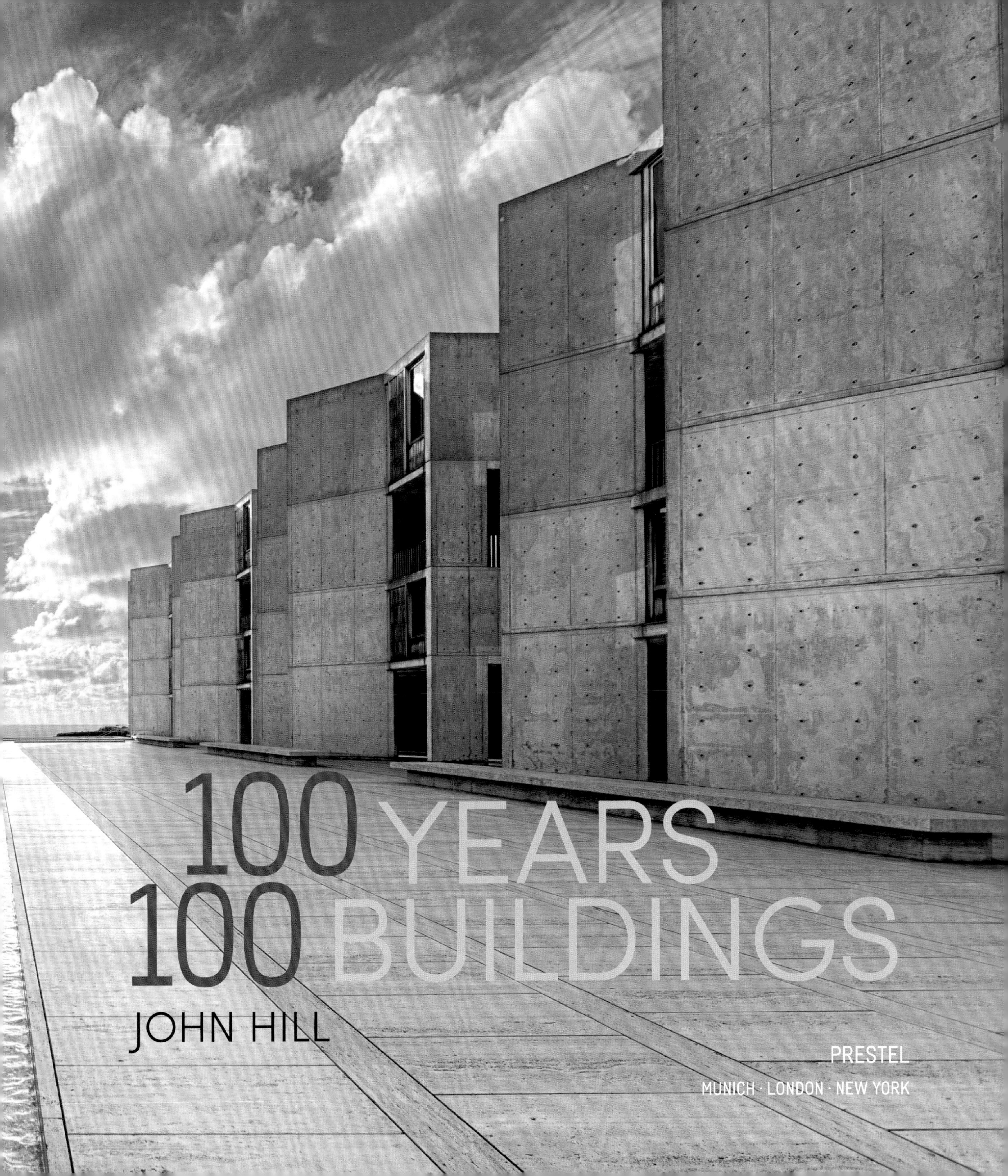

100 YEARS
100 BUILDINGS

JOHN HILL

PRESTEL

MUNICH · LONDON · NEW YORK

© Prestel Verlag, Munich · London · New York 2016
A member of Verlagsgruppe Random House GmbH
Neumarkter Strasse 28 · 81673 Munich

Prestel Publishing Ltd.
14-17 Wells Street
London W1T 3PD

Prestel Publishing
900 Broadway, Suite 603
New York, NY 10003

Library of Congress Cataloging-in-Publication Data
Names: Hill, John, 1973– author.
Title: 100 years 100 buildings / John Hill.
Other titles: One hundred years one hundred buildings
Description: Munich ; London ; New York : Prestel,
2016. | Includes bibliographical references.
Identifiers: LCCN 2016013527 | ISBN 9783791382128
Subjects: LCSH: Architecture, Modern—20th century. |
Architecture, Modern—21st century.
Classification: LCC NA680 .H46 2016 | DDC 724/.6—dc23
LC record available at http://lccn.loc.gov/2016013527

A CIP catalogue record for this book is available from
the British Library.

Editorial direction: Holly La Due
Design and layout: Laura Lindgren Design
Production management: Luke Chase
Copyediting: John Son
Proofreading: Kelli Rae Patton

Case binding: Detail, interior, Guggenheim Bilbao
by Frank Gehry, Bilbao, Spain (see p. 174)

Pages 2–3: Salk Institute by Louis I. Kahn,
San Diego, California, United States (see p. 111)

Pages 4–5: Detail, interior, Fundação Iberê Camargo
by Álvaro Siza, Porto Alegre, Brazil (see p. 196)

Page 6: Bloch Building, Nelson-Atkins Museum
of Art by Steven Holl Architects, Kansas City,
Missouri, United States (see p. 194)

Printed on the FSC -certified paper Chinese
Chenming Snow Eagle FSC matt art

Printed in China

ISBN 978-3-7913-8212-8

www.prestel.com

CONTENTS

INTRODUCTION

This book is an experiment of sorts. It presents one hundred buildings completed in the past hundred years—one building per year from 1916 to 2015. From the moment I decided to tackle the year-by-year format, the goal was to create a list of one hundred must-see buildings that truly spanned one hundred years, that didn't cluster in particular times. I knew the task would be difficult, but I also knew it would result in a balanced list of well-known icons, some lesser-known gems, and much in between.

Selecting only one great building per calendar year—based on date of completion, opening, inauguration, or some other criterion—means this book isn't simply a "100 best of" compilation of buildings; after all, the best buildings in that period theoretically could fall on a handful of dates. Therefore, this book uses the unique year-by-year format to accomplish a few things: it follows the ebbs and flows of style, technology, material, and other trends over the past hundred years; it aligns the buildings with contemporaneous events within and beyond architecture; and it calls attention to the myriad particular ways of designing buildings.

TRENDS

In history books, architecture is taught as a succession of styles. Although I cannot deny the role of style in making sense of architecture, that particular perspective is not this book's overriding concern. Often labeled well after the fact by historians and critics, style is secondary to the creation of architecture. Regardless, I'll admit architecture has moved through a number of styles in the last hundred years, most generally from Modernism between the World Wars, to postmodernism as a reaction to it in the 1970s, to the Deconstructivist label generated by the Museum of Modern Art in the late 1980s, to what could now be called, for lack of a better term, Pluralism. These large umbrella styles can be further broken down into smaller stylistic subsets, such as Expressionism, International Style, Brutalism, Critical Regionalism, High-Tech, Blobitecture, Parametricism, and so forth. Rather than focusing on the way buildings have been shaped stylistically over time by presenting at least one building from each stylistic strand, I hone in on how architects utilize context, technology, material, and even concept to shape space and therefore affect experience.

EVENTS

In terms of events outside of architecture, the past hundred years have been a series of crises of varying degrees: the two World Wars, the Great Depression, the Vietnam War, the energy crisis, the rise of neoliberalism, the fall of Communism, 9/11, globalization, and global warming, to name just a few from my admittedly Western perspective. Although the buildings in this book do not address all of these and other crises, the relationship between architecture and external events is obvious, yet worth stating explicitly: architecture is part of the world and is therefore affected by it, in turn impacting things outside of it.

Aside from world-changing events, architecture is ultimately at the service of society, so the role of architecture relative to it over the past century is evident in the types of buildings presented. Religious buildings are clustered toward the 1920s, for example, while museums are found in abundance closer to the present, indicating a shift in cultural values, among other external factors.

WAYS OF DESIGNING

Although the above two considerations might point to it, *100 Years, 100 Buildings* is not a history of architecture over the past hundred years. By focusing on individual buildings, this book functions like one hundred miniature case studies or, more accurately, introductions to one hundred buildings that encourage people to visit them, calling attention to the nuances of each project, the details of their creation, and the unique aspects of each design. Every building can be regarded relative to style, technique, or contextual event(s), but the circumstances of their creation are unique, and those circumstances are what this book is all about.

SELECTION CRITERIA

How then was the selection of buildings made? While the selection expresses my personal tastes, preferences, and values about what makes great architecture—and certain shortcomings, which will be explained below—there are three fairly objective criteria that were implemented in making the one-building-per-year selection:

First, the buildings are, well, buildings. This book defines architecture as the creation of spaces for human occupation. Therefore the focus is on spaces for living, working, learning, traveling, playing, and even grieving, but the selection also acknowledges the creation of urban space, or how a building fits into its context. This criterion eliminates projects that are, for example, landscapes, bridges, monuments or follies, even as the characteristics of these and other types of design may be present in the book, such as in buildings with strong landscape components or even a house that bridges a river.

Second, the buildings are extant. Architectural highlights from the years 1916 to 2015 could easily include never-built projects and buildings that were demolished or built as temporary structures. But I want this book to be an impetus for people to visit the buildings, to see them in context and sense the spaces as fully as possible. To do so, the buildings must be standing.

Third, the buildings are, to some degree, public. This criterion is important given the above emphasis on actually visiting buildings, yet it does not mean that all of the buildings are public institutions. Rather, each building selected is publicly accessible and/or makes a significant contribution to the public realm. Given the large span of time covered, this book then incorporates single-family residences from the early part of the twentieth century—what now are considered "house museums"—along with museums and other public institutions closer to the present.

Even with these three means of narrowing down buildings for consideration, the final selection was a highly subjective undertaking based on my experiences as an architect and writer about architecture. I'll be the first to admit the selection embodies some of the usual shortcomings that plague architectural publishing, namely a Western geographic leaning (forty-five buildings are in Europe, thirty in North America, eleven in South America, ten in Asia, three in Australia, and only one building in Africa), a preference for "name" architects, and a shortage of women architects. Much change has happened in the past one hundred years, but the attention given to buildings outside of the strongholds of Europe and the United States, to young and in many cases collaborative practices all over the world, and to the diversification of the male-dominated (white) profession is a fairly recent phenomenon. Evidence can be found, for example, in the six women architects found in the book's last ten buildings, versus only five (one of them a repeat) from the preceding ninety years!

These deficiencies are inadvertent, the product of a preference for modern architecture (which really began in the West early last century and then spread to all parts of the globe after WWII), a need to include the important icons of a few modern masters alongside lesser-known works, and, as noted, the year-by-year format. In regard to the last, it should be noted that determining when the buildings were completed was a tricky affair at times, given that many dates were surprisingly hard to pin down, with different dates coming from different sources (in some instances, the same source!). Establishing dates required some finessing in terms of nailing down the "correct" date (the reasoning and/or sources for the dates are spelled out in each building's description), but it also added an element of chance to the selection, such that a great building might have made the cut one particular year but not the year before or after. For these and other reasons, readers will no doubt find room for disagreement with both what is included as well as with what is omitted; in regard to the latter, up to four runners-up per year are listed as part of a time line of architecture culture at the back of the book, illustrating the difficulties confronted in the process and the plethora of great buildings also worth visiting.

THEMES DISCOVERED

Finally, with the selection being a synthesis of the objective criteria described above, my subjective judgments, and the year-by-year format, the resulting list opens itself up to the discovery of thematic strands. Below are a few of the more evident themes that I discovered, though by far they do not encompass every building in the book or all the possible commonalities among the buildings.

First-Time Freshness: With so much importance given to novelty and innovation in modern and contemporary architecture, it's no surprise that many outstanding buildings in these pages were an architect's first built project before they went on to become notable names and go-to architects later in life. Erich Mendelsohn's Einsteinturm (1921), R. M. Schindler's own house (1922), Moshe Safdie's Habitat 67 (1967), and Zaha Hadid's Vitra Fire Station (1993) are a few examples of young architects exploring new ideas and forms through their early buildings.

Building Overseas: At least since the diaspora of European architects in the 1930s, the profession of architecture has been global, with architects designing buildings for places well beyond their homes. With global telecommunications and air travel having dissolved the usual boundaries of place, this kind of work is more commonplace, witnessed by a few examples: Le Corbusier's Mill Owners' Association Building (1954) in India, Jørn Utzon's Sydney Opera House (1973) in Australia, Frank Gehry's Guggenheim Museum Bilbao (1997) in Spain, and Rem Koolhaas and OMA's CCTV Headquarters (2012) in China.

The Importance of Context: This will be an obvious point for architects, since any building responds to its context in myriad ways, be it climatic, social, political, cultural, or economic. Yet the best buildings manage to find creative and unexpected ways to build upon the history and/or natural features of a place while also creating something that shifts the context in a wholly new direction: Frank Lloyd Wright's decision to build Fallingwater (1938) over a waterfall; Ludwig Mies van der Rohe's Seagram Building (1958), which led to a revision of New York's zoning code; and James Stirling's Neue Staatsgalerie (1984), which re-created Stuttgart's pedestrian network in miniature.

Preserving Innovation: Modern and contemporary architecture tends to favor innovation over preservation, but as buildings of the early- to mid-twentieth century are confronted with the choice of preservation or demolition, preservation is one means of determining what buildings are valuable historically as well as in the present. Many of the buildings in this book have already been restored, renovated, or added onto in one way or another, thanks to enlightened owners and/or preservation advocates.

PROGNOSTICATION

With this last theme of preservation, the more recent buildings in the book could be seen as my candidates for preservation in the future. It's then interesting to hypothetically consider a version of this hundred-buildings-in-hundred-years book in fifty years' time (1966–2065). Would the buildings in the last half still merit inclusion? Only time will tell, and I'll leave it to the rest of this book to argue for the merits of each building, but it's safe to say that in looking forward certain trends will continue while others will fade away. The facts of diversity, brought up earlier, will impact not only who designs buildings but also who commissions the buildings and where they will be built. With a global projection of ten billion people in the year 2065, the social consciousness that has come to the fore in academia and the profession in recent years will (hopefully) increase, to be applied to housing and other buildings for communities not traditionally served by architects. Cultural buildings, the majority in the last quarter of this book, will continue, but in forms that embrace preservation and other sustainable practices rather than the creation of icons. Whatever the who, what, where, and how are in fifty years' time, I predict architecture will still be a spatial practice, the means of elevating our life experiences in ways unimagined—hopefully to the inclusion and benefit of as many people in as many places as possible.

1916 HOLLAND HOUSE

Hendrik Petrus Berlage ▸ London, England

The west facade on Bury Street. The building appears solid on approach, due to the narrow street and tightly spaced piers, an effect partially lost since the construction of 30 St. Mary Axe and its plaza across the street.

In addition to its architectural merits, as explained below, the first building selected in *100 Years, 100 Buildings* is exceptional for actually being completed in the midst of the First World War. H. P. Berlage (1856–1934), architect of the great Beurs van Berlage in Amsterdam (1903), designed the building for W. H. Müller & Co., a Dutch shipping company that operated a ferry service for freight and passengers between Rotterdam and London starting in the late 1800s. The building's most recognizable feature, its vertical lines of green glazed terra-cotta bricks, was manufactured in Delft and sent to London on the company's ships, a voyage aided by Dutch neutrality and the company's prioritizing the building's supplies over other shipments. The distinction of the bricks is due in part to their color, a dingy green that fits into London's gray and smoggy atmosphere, but also to their tight spacing and tapered profile.

Facing both south and west onto Bury Street, the facades give the impression of a solid, striped mass due to the narrow approach of the L-shaped street. With the completion of Norman Foster's 30 St. Mary Axe in 2004, this effect was obliterated on Holland House's more prominent west elevation by the construction of a new plaza that opened up a previously unavailable head-on view. The decorated spandrel panels, also in glazed terra-cotta, are now more pronounced, as is Foster's "Gherkin" reflected in the windows. The oblique appeal of the piers is heightened by the bricks' profiles, which start blocky right above the black granite base and then taper in successive steps toward the top of the six-story building. This subtle narrowing of the glazed piers gives the impression that they are load-bearing; in reality they conceal Holland House's other exceptional trait: its steel structure.

Considered the first steel-framed building in Europe, the structure was inspired by the buildings of Louis Sullivan in the United States, which Berlage saw firsthand in 1911. Much as Sullivan and other "Chicago School" architects emphasized the verticality of their steel-frame commercial buildings, Berlage's Holland House gave London a modern classic rich in detail and texture.

1917 CRYPT OF THE COLÒNIA GÜELL

Antoni Gaudí ▸ **Barcelona, Spain**

Interior view of the crypt and altar. In addition to the architecture in brick and stone, Antoni Gaudí designed the benches of wood and wrought iron—initially without kneelers, so that worshippers would pray with their knees on the concrete floor.

Architecture is a unique discipline in that many buildings often outlast their creators, surviving them and transforming themselves over time with different owners, renovations, additions, and the like. For Catalan architect Antoni Gaudí (1852–1926), his most famous building, the Sagrada Familia church in Barcelona, is projected to be complete in 2026, exactly one hundred years after his death. This time frame—144 years from the 1882 groundbreaking—is appropriate for, say, Gothic buildings, but it is exceptional in our modern age. With all the warranted attention given to the church's structure, design, and construction, Gaudí's other buildings take on more importance, especially the crypt he built for longtime patron Eusebi Güell—without it, the Sagrada Familia would have taken on a completely different form.

In 1898 industrialist Güell commissioned Gaudí to design a church on his textile estate of Santa Coloma de Cervelló outside Barcelona. Only the crypt was built, but evidence of the church's design exists in a sketch of the exterior, its tower and central dome resembling a scaled-down Sagrada Familia. The similarity came from the wholly original technique Gaudí applied first at Colònia Güell and later at Sagrada Familia: buckshot-filled sacks hung on strings to create the catenary curves that, once inverted, approximated the final outlines of the churches. Unlike the Sagrada Familia, Gaudí did not build a plaster model of Güell's church, and the single surviving drawing did not provide enough information for anyone to complete the project once the space was blessed in 1915. By that year Gaudí had begun devoting all of his time to the Sagrada Familia, so another architect completed the crypt in 1917.

Tucked next to a hill on the estate, the entrance to the crypt is found through a hall of columns with their tops branching out like the surrounding pine trees. Inside, slanted columns of brick and basalt define the central nave and the U-shaped gallery around it. These columns reveal a subtle hint of the forces that would have been traveling down from the church above; that the church was not built meant structural problems eventually occurred, requiring restoration and a new roof many decades later. Other striking features of the interior include radial brick ribs above the nave and stained glass windows by Gaudí's longtime collaborator Josep Maria Jujol. Tiny by the standards of Gaudí's unfinished masterpiece in Barcelona, this crypt is a small space that is as delightful as it is prescient.

1918 HALLIDIE BUILDING

Willis Polk ▸ San Francisco, California, United States

Detail of the south facade. The glass wall cantilevered in front of the concrete structure is in striking contrast with its neighbor, which is more representative of the mix of glass and masonry built in early-twentieth-century office buildings.

Even with the rise of the so-called Chicago School in the 1880s and 1890s showcasing the potential of hanging large expanses of glass on steel frames, most early-twentieth-century buildings in US cities were well below 50-percent glass. Such was the case with the classically styled buildings designed by Willis Polk, who was actually associated with the firm of Chicago architect Daniel Burnham for about a decade. The Hallidie Building, then, with its full seven stories of clear glass, is an anomaly, an approach that would not catch on for at least another three decades.

Polk was hired by the University of California, Berkeley, in 1916 to design a building (named for cable car pioneer Andrew Smith Hallidie) on Sutter Street in downtown San Francisco as an investment for the school. Faced with budget limitations and a six-month construction schedule before the building's 1918 opening, he designed a concrete-frame building with an all-glass wall facing the south street for its natural light. The gridded curtain wall is hung one meter (3'3") in front of the columns by an upturned beam at the slab edge, and slender concrete cantilevers supported by tapered brackets. Four bands of ornamental ironwork run horizontally across the base and top of the building, terminating in fire escapes with curved profiles. Colored the university's blue and gold, these frilly edges indicate that Polk was unable to abandon history completely and did not know what to do architecturally with the new technology. Aesthetically the contrast is interesting as it highlights the impressive glass wall like a new painting in an old frame.

Deemed a city landmark in 1971, against the then-owner's wishes, the Hallidie Building underwent restoration in 1975. Yet by the beginning of the next century the facade was dull and deteriorated, and in 2010 it was deemed unsafe by a city building inspector. Preservation architects Page & Turnbull with McGinnis Chen Associates completed a major restoration of the glass walls, ornamental ironwork, and fire escapes in 2013. Looking brand new, and now appropriately home to the San Francisco chapter of the American Institute of Architects, among other tenants, the building is a combination of Polk's onetime Modernist expression and twenty-first-century building and preservation technology.

1919 HELSINKI CENTRAL RAILWAY STATION

Eliel Saarinen ▸ **Helsinki, Finland**

The station's ticket hall and waiting area. Following World War I and the building's use—and abuse—as a military hospital, Saarinen reconfigured the waiting room into its current state of elegance.

If at the beginning of the twenty-first century the airport was the most complex building typology in its integration of architecture, engineering, and infrastructure, more than a century earlier the same could be said of the railway terminal. The myriad strands of tracks leading to the station, the dense urban conditions where they were placed, and the desire to create a civic monument combined to make the railway terminal an enormously complicated undertaking. When Eliel Saarinen (1873–1950) and his partners Herman Gesellius and Armas Lindgren won the 1904 competition to replace Helsinki's outdated central railway station, critics found the National Romanticist style of their winning design out of touch with the modern aesthetic then developing in other parts of Europe. Saarinen responded with visits to stations in Britain and Germany in the years 1905–1907, by which time he practiced independently and developed a simplified redesign that brought the station's appearance closer to a daring competition entry by Sigurd Frosterus. This fairly abrupt about-face is seen as the beginning of modern architecture in Finland and the second phase of Saarinen's career, which would find fruition in the United States (see 1942).

The station has a monumental presence in central Helsinki thanks to its predominantly stone exterior and its location adjacent to a sizable square. A 160-foot-tall (49 m) clock tower topped by a copper roof faces the square on the east and "turns the corner" toward the entrance on the south. There the arched-window entrance is hard to miss: capped by a barrel-vaulted roof trimmed in copper, it is flanked by two pairs of oversize and stylized figures sculpted by Emil Wikström. While a hodgepodge of associations is evident—particularly the banks of Louis Sullivan and the work of Josef Hoffmann and Joseph Olbrich in Vienna— the exterior has a presence that is unmistakably Nordic, bridging the Finnish vernacular with the modern. The main space inside the entrance echoes the vaulted form, but the flanking halls (one for ticketing/waiting and one a fast-food chain) are more architecturally interesting. Here the curved ceiling—rendered in precast concrete—takes on a shallower profile to give the space some grandeur and elegance in concert with the green-tile piers.

Helsinki Central Railway Station was realized in two phases following the 1904 competition: the administration section (1905–1909) and the station proper (1910– 1914). Just as soon as it was completed the station was converted into a Russian military hospital for use during the Great War. It wasn't until 1919—two years after Finland gained independence from Russia—that the building finally opened as a railroad station, which it has remained ever since.

1920 HET SCHIP

Michel de Klerk ▸ Amsterdam, Netherlands

Detail of the facade and tower on Hembrugstraat. Michel de Klerk's powerhouse design of brick and tile culminates in the tower that rises from a two-story base on the north end of the triangular block.

In the second decade of the twentieth century, architect Michel de Klerk (1884–1923) designed and realized three projects for workers' housing on the Spaarndammerplantsoen, a small square in Amsterdam's Spaarndammerbuurt district. The first two projects, completed in 1915 and 1918, have long elevations that face the square on its north and south sides, but when it came time to fill out the eastern edge of the site, that commission went to government architects. Nevertheless, in appreciation of De Klerk's previous buildings, the head of the Municipal Housing Department hired him to work with the Eigen Haard Housing Association on a block that tangentially approaches the square on the west. The block's triangular shape, combined with De Klerk's distinctive "Amsterdam School" brickwork, earned the courtyard building its name (translation: "The Ship").

The project called for 102 dwellings, and De Klerk borrowed apartment plans from his two neighboring projects and positioned them along the long Zaanstraat and Oostzaanstraat frontages on the west and east, respectively. An existing school breaks up the Oostzaanstraat side, but in an effort to unify the whole block he added new floors to the school (realized posthumously) with complementary brickwork that overlaps the lower section to signal the entrance. Across the front of the five stories of apartments are orange-brick walls in thick bands divided by lines of tile that alternate between horizontal and vertical coursing. Bulges at the dark brick base indicate entrances, while those at the top floor give the building a meandering profile against the sky.

With much of the triangular block filled with these dwellings, the moments of difference are confined to the narrow tip of the block by Spaarndammerplantsoen and the Hembrugstraat frontage to the north. For the former, De Klerk designed a low post office (now housing the Museum Het Schip, which gives guided tours of the block) with a cylindrical tower set back from a small plaza that overlooks the square across the street. On Hembrugstraat to the north, he continued some of the standard dwellings around the corner from the east and west sides but hinted at the exclamation point mid-block in the bulbous "cigar" corners, an odd detail that is nevertheless playful and endearing. Halfway between these corner bulges is a small court created by angling the plan toward the middle of the block, and a slender tower whose curved sides taper to a point. The tower gives the block some added visibility in the area, but it also gives the block a strong civic presence, reiterated by the meeting hall that De Klerk designed for the courtyard, a public space in his day that was as informal and expressive as the exterior.

1921 EINSTEINTURM

Erich Mendelsohn ▸ Potsdam, Germany

In purely formal terms, Einsteinturm is an anomaly both within the evolution of modern architecture and in the oeuvre of its architect, Erich Mendelsohn (1887–1953). The clean lines, smooth surfaces, and generous glazing of International Style modernism became the default style for modern architecture in the ensuing decades, rather than anything approaching the tower's Expressionism. And Mendelsohn, who went on to realize many buildings over a long and fruitful career, never designed anything else quite like it. His subsequent buildings, like the De La Warr Pavilion (see 1935), with Serge Chermayeff in England, were more classically modern than sculpturally expressive. Yet all of his buildings were unique responses to site, program, and client, an approach rooted in Einsteinturm.

Mendelsohn spent part of World War I in the trenches, where he sketched factories, railway stations, and houses that appeared to be purely fantastical curvaceous structures, but which for him could be built someday. In this vein, he sketched what would become Einsteinturm, following some basic plans generated by his client, astronomer Erwin Finlay-Freundlich, who introduced the architect to Albert Einstein's general theory of relativity before the war. Finlay-Freundlich had wanted to build a solar observatory to test Einstein's theory (by observing light bent by gravity during an eclipse), but his efforts were thwarted by, among other things, the war. Not until the conflict came to its end was he able to move forward with the project and bring Germany's research facilities up to speed with those in the United States, England, and France.

For Mendelsohn, reinforced concrete was *the* material for creating the new postwar forms of architecture, and the tower was where he would realize it for the first time. Construction began in 1920, but only the basement, entrance, and cupola would be made of concrete, due to a postwar shortage. Dejected and without the time to redesign the tower for structural "honesty," he substituted brick and stucco for concrete, never using the materials in such a way again.

Although Mendesolhn's design was subsequently criticized most for its materiality, the expressive form—his attempt at representing the movement and energy underlying the general theory of relativity—encloses a fully functioning observatory, with the coelostat (rotating mirrors) in the tower, and labs in the basement. The building was completed in 1921, but it would be another three years for the telescope from Carl Zeiss and interior furnishings to be installed. In the late 1990s the tower underwent repairs, including updated mirrors and other equipment, and to this day it is still used as a solar observatory and a venue for special events in what is called, appropriately, the Albert Einstein Science Park.

1922 SCHINDLER HOUSE

Rudolph M. Schindler ▸ Los Angeles, California, United States

Interior of the Schindler studio. Fireplaces were provided inside, here between the glass walls opening on to the patio and the tilt-up concrete walls giving privacy from the neighboring buildings.

View of the Schindler patio. Each of the house's two patios was also provided with fireplaces.

Even though the men who designed early modern houses receive the recognition, a number of them owe their innovations, and therefore their lasting influence, to women. The house Gerrit Rietveld designed for Mrs. Truus Schröder-Schräder (see 1924) and the house Ludwig Mies van der Rohe designed for Dr. Edith Farnsworth (see 1951) are two examples found in *100 Years, 100 Buildings.* In the house R. M. Schindler (1887–1953) designed and lived in from 1922 until his death, that female influence was his wife, Sophie Pauline Gibling. With her collaboration, the Schindler House became influential as much for its social considerations as for its novel construction and integration of building and landscape.

Gibling wasn't the only woman involved in the project; her classmate Marian Chace was also a client, since the house was designed for the Schindlers as well as Marian and her husband, Clyde Chace. With a large site on Kings Road between Hollywood and Beverly Hills, Schindler developed what he described as "cooperative dwellings for two young couples." Private living quarters were provided for each couple, which included studios, open porches on the roof for sleeping, and patios on opposite sides of the house formed by the two L-shaped wings. Uniting the two one-story residences was a shared kitchen and fireplace, joined by a third L-shaped wing with a guest suite and garage. From the start, the house was as much a salon as a communal dwelling, its indoor and outdoor spaces as appropriate for large groups as for the two couples.

Two materials predominate in the building: concrete and wood. Concrete is used for the floors and the tilt-up walls—vertical on the inside, slightly battered on the outside—with their tilt-up construction accentuated by narrow slots of glass between them. Redwood makes up the ceilings and the framing for the doors and windows, the latter generously sized and literally opening up to the patios. Clerestory windows pop up from the low, overhanging flat roof to bring light deeper into the plan. This simple palette and its resulting spatial flow went on to influence and define much of what is considered Southern California residential architecture.

With help from Pauline Schindler, who divorced Schindler but lived in the Chace wing until he died, the nonprofit Friends of the Schindler House bought the house, which has been open to the public since 1980. In 1994 it entered an agreement with the MAK - Austrian Museum of Applied Arts / Contemporary Arts to create the MAK Center for Art and Architecture. To this day the MAK Center retains a version of the Schindler House's social dimension through exhibitions, events, and tours that include other Schindler buildings in the area that it owns.

1923 NOTRE DAME DU RAINCY

Auguste Perret ▸ **Raincy, France**

Church nave, looking west toward the altar. Echoes of the shapes of the concrete blocks holding the stained glass walls are found in the center of the nave, where the blocks are set into the reinforced concrete vault.

Auguste Perret (1874–1954) was a master artist and technician with reinforced concrete, applying the material to a variety of building types: museums, theaters, housing, and churches. With a consummate attention to detail, he crafted (always in collaboration with his brothers Claude and Gustave) surfaces with a complexity that bridged the traditional and the modern. He asserted that instead of covering concrete with stone or some other decorative material, it should be formed and finished to express its "spiritual qualities." In this regard Notre Dame du Raincy is the apotheosis of the Perret brothers' architectural explorations in concrete.

Located in Raincy, a suburb northeast of Paris, the church (a.k.a. Our Lady of Consolation) was built to commemorate those who died in World War I, specifically the September 1914 Battle of the Ourcq River, a bloody attack that helped stop the German advance on Paris. From the beginning, when the local priest commissioned the Perret brothers, economy was paramount due to limited funds; remarkably, they were able to deliver a sizable church built in only fourteen months (April 1922–June 1923). The church has a strong presence in its context thanks to a 145-foot-tall (44 m) tower facing east, but the appealing facets of the design are found behind the stark gray exterior.

At the behest of Perret's patron, Abbé Nègre, Notre Dame du Raincy's floor plan is simple, a single rectangular, basilica-like 63 × 185 foot (19 × 56 m) space with side aisles formed by two rows of columns. As a reflection of the budgetary constraints, the floor of the nave follows the existing grade of the site, which slopes down toward the altar raised atop steps that extend across the width of the space. Stained glass windows wrap all four sides, flooding the space in color and drawing comparisons to Gothic cathedrals. Yet three details distinguish Perret's modern church from its Gothic predecessors: first, the stained glass, executed by Marguérite Huré, is inserted into open concrete blocks of different shapes (circle, cross, diamond, etc.) that prioritize pattern over the occasional symbolism (also, the color has a noticeable gradient from yellow and green at the entrance to blue and purple at the altar); second, the concrete roof is formed in shallow vaults instead of groin vaults, with the side aisles and nave running perpendicular to each other; and third, the convex-fluted columns in concrete are slender, with the outer rows detached from the exterior wall to reiterate the freedom of the exterior wall from the structure. These details combine to create a space of exuberance completely formed by concrete, which Perret and his brothers turned into a spiritual material of the highest order.

1924 RIETVELD SCHRÖDER HOUSE

Gerrit Rietveld ▸ Utrecht, Netherlands

Top floor with the walls open. Even when completely open, the location of the sliding walls upstairs can be grasped by the lines of primary colors on the ceiling.

House exterior seen from the southeast. Fearing resistance to the modern design when obtaining a building permit, Rietveld drew the east elevation (right) with the profile of the neighboring house behind it, as if they were one and the same.

When it comes to great buildings, architects receive most of the praise—be they individuals or firms—but in some cases, much, if not most of the credit, is due the client. Great clients can bring out an architect's best work by equally embracing and challenging their talents. Truus Schröder-Schräder was one such client.

After her husband died in 1923, Schröder-Schräder hired Dutch architect and designer Gerrit Rietveld (1888–1964) to design a small house for her and her three children (Rietveld had earlier designed a modern room for her in the Schröder family's nineteenth-century house). Initially desiring a place in Amsterdam, away from the memories of her late husband, she opted to stay in Utrecht after both she and Rietveld discovered separately over the same weekend an ideal lot facing a polder on what was then the edge of the city (a highway now separates the house and polder). She desired independence, rationality, and transparency in the house, while he wanted to break free of domestic and architectural associations through the use of primary forms, shapes, and color. The built result, considered the best example of the short-lived De Stijl movement, is like a building-scale expression of his revolutionary chairs (or the paintings of fellow De Stijl member Piet Mondrian), showing that "the style" could bridge different scales and functions.

But the building was far from the masterpiece it's recognized as today when Rietveld first put pencil to paper. When he didn't deliver on Schröder-Schräder's progressive ideals in his first scheme, she pushed him to go further, and his final design is the result of their mutually respectful relationship. Points, lines, and planes overlap and unite into a complex and asymmetrical, yet balanced exterior that appears arbitrary but directly relates to the interior layout. The ground floor contains five traditionally partitioned rooms, each with a door to the outside and one used by Rietveld as an office, then a living quarters late in life. Up a central stair is the free-flowing, flexible living space the house is known for, where three sliding walls can be arranged to create one large open space, five small rooms, or any combination in-between.

In 1970, six years after Rietveld died, Schröder-Schräder created the Rietveld Schröder House Foundation for the preservation and celebration of the architect's work. Shortly thereafter the house was skillfully restored to its original state, which involved a number of interior re-creations. Since 1987 the house has been open to the public, run by the Centraal Museum Utrecht. Less shocking today than when Schröder-Schräder moved in at the end of 1924, the colorful house still exudes the experimental qualities she strove for and which Rietveld delivered.

1925 PAVILLON DE L'ESPRIT NOUVEAU

Le Corbusier ▸ **Bologna, Italy**

The pavilion seen from the southeast. The pavilion in Bologna is an exact replica of the Parisian original, down to the mural on the side and a tree piercing the roof in the courtyard.

Le Corbusier (1887–1965, born Charles-Édouard Jeanneret-Gris) is considered one of the three most influential architects of the twentieth century, alongside Ludwig Mies van der Rohe and Frank Lloyd Wright. The Swiss-born French architect embraced industrialization and modernization, and he found suitable expression in the houses—the oft-quoted "machines for living in"—he designed during the 1920s and 1930s. While the formal influence of this purist phase of his work remains to this day, the same cannot be said for the urban planning proposals he developed during the same period. Most famously, in his 1925 Plan Voisin proposal, he envisioned a large swath of the Right Bank of Paris wiped out in favor of a grid of towers set on superblocks, which critics later blamed for the disastrous urban renewal projects of the mid-twentieth century.

The Pavillon de l'Esprit Nouveau, designed for the 1925 International Exposition of Modern Industrial and Decorative Arts in Paris, became a lasting symbol of these two strands of Le Corbusier's work. With its white walls, large windows, open plan, and industrial furnishings (what he called "equipment"), the pavilion was a jarring dose of the avant-garde among the fancifully decorated pavilions that littered the Champs de Mars and Trocadéro on both sides of the Eiffel Tower. His expression of a house for the people rather than for the rich was not embraced enthusiastically by the fair's organizers, so they relegated the pavilion to a remote patch of land filled with trees; in turn, the pavilion included a courtyard pierced by one of the trees. On display, the pavilion's rectilinear volume presented this new way of living at a 1:1 scale, while the rounded volume exhibited his Plan Voisin, which must have shocked the fair's spectators more than the living spaces free of ornament and equipped with furniture supplied typically to hospitals.

Yet how is a temporary pavilion at a world's fair lasting? In 1977, under the guidance of architects Giuliano Gresleri and Jose Oubrerie, the Pavillon de l'Esprit Nouveau was rebuilt in Bologna's Fair district. A lonely presence on a green space surrounded by roads and parking, the pavilion is run by Emilia-Romagna IBC (Istituto per i beni artistici culturali e naturali) and is accessible by appointment. Gladly, some young architects in the city have explored ways of making it more publicly accessible and a less unknown presence in the city, giving it a new life nearly a century after it was designed.

1926 BAUHAUS DESSAU

Walter Gropius ▸ Dessau, Germany

The *Prellerhaus* block seen from the east. The twenty-eight studios in the six-story building added a dimension of communal living to the Bauhaus's pedagogical program.

The workshop block seen from the southwest. The signature view of the Bauhaus shows the three-story curtain wall hung off the concrete structure, its transparency accentuated by glass corners.

Remarkably, one of the most influential modern buildings ever built, and the most impressive built manifestation of a school whose name is synonymous with a recognizable style and progressive design education, the Bauhaus building in Dessau was in use for only six years. The school itself lasted a bit longer, from its founding in 1919 to its closure in 1933 after the Nazis came to power. Upon its closing, a who's who of progressive architects, artists, and designers—"Bauhauslers" Josef Albers, Marcel Breuer, Walter Gropius, László Moholy-Nagy, and Ludwig Mies van der Rohe, among others—departed for other countries and schools, carrying the Bauhaus ideals with them and lengthening the reach of the school's influence.

The school's long-lasting impact would be hard to imagine without the building Bauhaus founder Walter Gropius (1883–1969) designed in 1926. Dessau mayor Fritz Hesse offered the Bauhaus money, patronage, intellectual freedom, as well as land and funding, for a new building with housing, all in the name of modernization. Gropius immediately faced two major challenges in relation to the site and the program itself: a planned roadway ran through the property, and the building needed to incorporate a technical college. His response was a plan with three wings, one of which was devoted to the technical college, reached by a bridge containing two floors of offices that spanned the road. The other blocks included a one-story "festive area" (canteen and auditorium) with six floors of studios (dormitory, called the *Prellerhaus*) and a four-story workshop block. Given the school's emphasis on research and practice, with workshops prevailing over traditional classrooms, the workshop block was the building's signature expression, its three above-grade floors covered with fully glazed curtain walls well before they would become ubiquitous.

Following the Bauhaus's closure in 1933, the building was used for two years as a state women's school. The building was damaged in 1945 during an air raid, even though the signature whitewashed walls were camouflaged with brown paint, the roof was painted black and the windows were coated with antiglare paint. Deemed a historical monument in the 1960s, the building was restored and reconstructed the following decade, but with details that departed severely from the original. A decadelong restoration that finished in 2011 stayed truer to the original (even finding original windows used in greenhouses scattered about Dessau), and also improved the building's previously deplorable thermal performance. Run by the Bauhaus Dessau Foundation since 1994, the building is open to the public with a permanent exhibition on modern design and the chance to "sleep like a Bauhausler" in the *Prellerhaus*.

1927 GRUNDTVIGS KIRKE

Peder Vilhelm Jensen-Klint ▸ Copenhagen, Denmark

West elevation. P. V. Jensen-Klint's fusion of the Dutch village churches he had studied with Gothic cathedrals was in no place more evident than the massive church front rising the equivalent of sixteen stories.

One of the church's two side aisles. The use of bricks, a humble building material, throughout gives the Gothic-styled church a modern minimalism that parallels Grundtvig's writings and teachings on nature, freedom, and education.

In 1913, one year after P. V. Jensen-Klint (1853–1930) failed, alongside every other competitor, to win a competition for the Grundtvig Memorial Hall in Copenhagen, he won the follow-up competition for a memorial to priest, writer, and educator Nikolaj Frederik Severin Grundtvig (1783–1872) with his design of Grundtvigs Kirke. Actually, Jensen-Klint won second prize behind sculptor Niels Hansen Jacobsen, but a member of the jury—a former classmate of Jensen-Klint—disagreed vehemently with the decision and persuaded the rest of the jury to change their minds. Finally, Jensen-Klint was no longer resigned to having his designs linger on paper as "castles in the air," as he called the numerous churches and other buildings he had dreamed up since the middle of the previous decade. Other churches he designed would be completed before the bell tower and the nave of Grundtvigs Kirke in 1940, but the Tower Church, as the huge bell tower was called, was consecrated on December 11, 1927; by then the power of Jensen-Klint's masterpiece in brick was already apparent.

An exceptional thing to consider with Grundtvigs Kirke was that instead of trying to fit the sizable church into an existing urban context, it was sited in the open with the context planned around it. Once the then-unpopulated Bispebjerg Hill was selected, Jensen-Klint designed housing to wrap around the church and turn it into what he called "the town on the hill." Most dramatically, he placed a street lined with row houses on the western axis, framing the wide tower with its vertical stripes and stepped gables rising to 160 feet (49 m).

Consistent among the housing, the church, and most of the town on the hill was brick, specifically a cream-yellow brick made in Zealand. More than five million were used to build the church's crypt, tower, and nave. Although time and the elements have given the exterior bricks a gray tinge (complementing the red tile roofs very well), the church's creamy interior is the same now as it was half a century ago. Bricks in standard sizes, as well as custom shapes formed by cutting and polishing, cover every visible surface in the church—columns, walls, vaults, and floors—but they are also at the core of the structure, holding up the church and pushing it heavenward.

After Jensen-Klint's death in 1930 (his funeral was in the unfinished yet partially enclosed nave), his son Kaare Klint completed the church, which included designs for the large pulpit, altar, chairs, and organ on the north wall. His son, Jensen-Klint's grandson, Esben Klint, designed the large western organ and the chandeliers. In the end, three generations of Klint architects utilized one building material that when multiplied five million times equaled tranquility.

1928 GOETHEANUM

Rudolf Steiner ▸ Dornach, Switzerland

No space inside is more sculptural than the west stair, crisscrossed by steps and landings on the way to the main hall.

The Geotheanum's west end. The building sits atop a hill, so it looks upon the surrounding buildings that echo the Goetheanum's sculptural form.

The Goetheanum that Rudolf Steiner (1861–1925) built in Dornach, a small town near Basel, stands as an architectural anomaly. For one thing, although Steiner considered himself an architect, he was more established as a philosopher, an author, an editor, and the founder of anthroposophy, a movement that aimed for inner development through the mutual influences of nature and what he coined "spiritual science." Also, it is formally distinct from traditional and avant-garde styles of the time. Though the Goetheanum did not see completion in his lifetime, it remains a one-of-a-kind building that arguably expresses the beliefs of its creator more clearly than any other building in early-twentieth-century architecture.

Actually, the Goetheanum cannot literally be called one of a kind since it is the second such building on the Dornach site donated to Steiner. Following his founding of the Anthroposophical Society in 1912, Steiner set about creating the first Goetheanum, a theater named for Johann Wolfgang von Goethe, whose books Steiner edited and whose scientific views on nature he admired greatly. Although Steiner envisioned his organic, no-straight-lines architecture in concrete, the society members convinced him to build the first iteration out of wood (he was able to build some of the surrounding smaller structures with his material of choice, such as an unabashedly phallic steam plant). On New Year's Eve 1922, ten years after construction started, the first Goetheanum was destroyed by fire. One year later Steiner vowed to rebuild—in concrete.

Construction of the second Goetheanum began in 1924 and it opened in 1928, still unfinished; it would take more than thirty years for all of the interior spaces to be completed (the Great Hall was finished only in 1957 after a design competition was held). Although Steiner wanted a unique appearance for the second Goetheanum, it resembles the first in its sculptural plasticity and formal symmetry, but departs from it in size (being much bigger than the first), and the omission of a dome (even without one, it holds a commanding presence from its hilltop site). The sculpted concrete walls on the exterior fold into each other like a meringue, while at the roof they flare out to give the massive building its distinctive flowering appearance. Behind the concrete walls are two theaters, including the Great Hall at the building's center. But the architectural highlight is the stair hall on the west, a complex space bathed in light from a large window decorated by Steiner. Although this side of the Goetheanum wasn't completed until 1964, those architects wisely left the stair's Piranesian construction of zigzagging concrete steps and arching supports in its original state. Ascending the stair is like taking a trip inside Rudolf Steiner's esoteric brain.

1929 BARCELONA PAVILION

Ludwig Mies van der Rohe ▸ Barcelona, Spain

The north pool. Mies appreciated Georg Kolbe's *Dawn* figure so much he used another Kolbe sculpture in the Berlin Building Exhibition in 1931.

Looking toward the pool on the north. The onyx wall seen on end serves an important spatial function, but it also hides one of the necessary roof drains.

If not for the reconstruction of the German Pavilion—better known as the Barcelona Pavilion—the most lasting physical artifact of the 1929 Barcelona International Exposition would be the Barcelona chair designed by Ludwig Mies van der Rohe (1886–1969), who did not want anything heavy or ornamental clashing with his minimalist architectural vision. Eventually mass-produced, the iconic chair would go on to grace the lobbies of nearly every modern office building since. His pavilion, on the other hand, existed only in photographs and words from 1930 until 1986, when its reconstruction allowed new generations of admirers to experience what in its day was a revolutionary way of creating architecture and space.

Less than a year before the expo's opening day, Mies was selected to design the national pavilion for Germany along with its exhibits; his longtime collaborator Lilly Reich handled the latter. Free of any function outside of the inaugural festivities, Mies designed the pavilion as a statement of the new, modern architecture, but also of the spirit of the liberal and democratic Weimar Republic. Situated on a cross-axis with the Magic Fountain of Montjuïc, the pavilion was as much a space to move through as a destination. And moving through it provided an experience unlike any other building of the time, with no direct route through the pavilion and the blurring of distinctions between inside and outside.

This ambiguity, even today, arises from the way Mies handled the structure and enclosure as separate elements. A grid of eight cruciform, stainless-steel-covered columns supports the roof, with most columns close to but not engaging the pavilion's walls. These walls—composed of onyx, five types of marble, and three types of glass—define the spaces between the white roof and travertine paving, but their varied reflections, colors, and patterns add a complexity that belies the plan's free-flowing, minimal strokes. The pools on either side of the covered spaces provide further reflections: a large, light-green pool out in the open and a small dark pool embraced by three marble walls. Georg Kolbe's sculpture *Dawn* stands in one corner of the small pool, terminating a vista from the western garden edge. Although at odds with the abstraction prevalent in the pavilion, the sculpture is a perfect melding of art and architecture, such that the reconstruction would have been incomplete without it.

The Barcelona Pavilion is run by the Mies van der Rohe Foundation, which organizes awards, conferences, exhibitions, workshops, and installations, some of them taking place at the pavilion. More than fifty years after its original completion, the Barcelona Pavilion has a purpose that is much more than just a place to sit on Mies's iconic chair.

1930 VILLA TUGENDHAT

Ludwig Mies van der Rohe ▸ Brno, Czech Republic

Living space and conservatory. The onyx wall on the right splits the living space into two, while curtains on tracks provide more privacy.

Rear elevation seen from the west. The awning is visible above the living space's long glass wall, which retracts into the basement.

Like many German architects who practiced between the two World Wars, Ludwig Mies van der Rohe's (1886–1969) career spans two halves: his work in Europe and his work in the United States. Of the European houses he designed, all but two were built in Germany: the Wolf House (1927), considered his first modern house, built predominantly out of brick in Gubin, Poland, eventually destroyed by bombing in the war; and the Tugendhat House, designed and built for Grete and Fritz Tugendhat.

Grete (née Löw-Beer) came from a well-to-do Jewish family of industrialists who gave her and Fritz a large sloping plot of land when they married in 1928. That same year they met Mies through a friend and hired him for a large, five-bedroom house. He responded by the end of the year with a split-level, three-story plan (two living floors plus a partial basement) that was predominantly closed on the street elevation but open through large expanses of glass on the garden elevation. The entire structure was framed in steel, unheard of at the time. Upstairs were the garage and chauffeur's quarters in one volume, and the entrance and the five bedrooms in another (a gap between framed a view to the garden), while downstairs were the huge open living space, library, dining room, and kitchen. The Tugendhats liked the plan and only asked for three minor revisions that Mies complied with, resulting in one of the greatest modern houses of the twentieth century.

One way to examine the house is to look, as Mies was wont to do, at the details, which were highly considered and well executed, from the street entrance to the living space overlooking the garden; the cruciform column holding up the entrance canopy; translucent glass panes lining the curved stair; the travertine floor leading downstairs; the onyx wall separating the living room into two zones; ebony panels lining the library and dining room; cruciform columns covered in chrome; retractable awnings shading the living space; and finally the large glass panes that lower into the basement, literally opening up the house to the garden.

Although the home was a fitting place for the Tugendhats and their three children, the family would remain in the house only eight years after its completion, forced to flee to Switzerland in 1938. The Nazis confiscated the house and used it as an office for aviation engineers during the war. Later it was turned into a eurythmics school and a branch of the nearby children's hospital. Now owned by the city of Brno and open to the public, Villa Tugendhat was most recently restored in 2012, returning its lush materials and details to a state that is easy to appreciate.

1931 VILLA SAVOYE

Le Corbusier ▸ Poissy, France

The living space and roof terrace. The ribbon windows wrap all sides of the house, regardless of function or location, inside or outside.

The elevation facing northwest. The object in the landscape is the ultimate expression of Le Corbusier's Five Points of Architecture, all visible from the garden.

Even before laying eyes directly on Villa Savoye, its presence can be felt in its small gatehouse near the road. In this "mini-Savoye," three of Le Corbusier's (1887–1965) famous Five Points of Architecture are readily visible: the top floor of the two-story structure is lifted upon *pilotis*; the walls of the ground floor are placed free of the structure and the walls above; and one side of the upper floor features a horizontal ribbon window. All that is missing are the free design of the facade in front of the structure and the roof garden; to see these one just needs to follow the driveway toward the house surrounded by trees.

Pierre and Emilie Savoye hired Le Corbusier to design a weekend house with servants' quarters in Poissy, a country town that is now a western suburb of Paris. Given that the Savoyes drove to the villa on weekends, the aforementioned driveway continues under the main floor in a horseshoe shape that winds between the *pilotis* supporting the upper floor and the (now) dark-green curved walls of the ground floor, and ends at the three-car garage adjacent to the servants' quarters. Upstairs, the almost square *piano nobile's* living room, bedrooms, and terrace are wrapped in ribbon windows that embrace views in all directions. The roof is given over to a solarium behind undulating walls pierced by a rectangular opening that frames a view of the countryside.

The plan of each level is so distinct that they don't seem to be part of the same house. But centering each plan is a ramp that brilliantly connects all three floors through a *promenade architecturale* that rises from dark to light and from inside to outside, culminating in the framed rooftop view. Yes, there is a spiral stair (to have been used primarily by servants), but the back-and-forth ramp cuts across the indoor and outdoor spaces of the house to orient people within the house as well as the landscape.

As an architectural statement of Le Corbusier's Five Points, the Villa Savoye worked admirably, but as a weekend house it was not without its problems. It leaked, was cold, and was abandoned after less than a decade, right before World War II. In the late 1950s the town of Poissy considered razing the villa, which was used to store hay during the war and decayed considerably in the ensuing years. But opposition from architects, including Le Corbusier himself, led to its protection as a landmark and a restoration that ended in 1997. The villa is currently run by the Centre des monuments nationaux and open to the public.

1932 PSFS BUILDING

Howe and Lescaze ▸ Philadelphia, Pennsylvania, United States

Market Street elevation. The hotel lobby, formerly the PSFS banking hall, sits behind an exterior with polished granite and a large window turning a rounded corner.

At only 32 stories and not quite 500 feet (150 m) tall to its roof (750 feet [228 m] to the tip of its antenna), the tower of the Philadelphia Savings Fund Society (PSFS) built at Twelfth and Market Streets in downtown Philadelphia is substantially shorter than two more-famous towers realized in those lean Depression years: the spire of the 103-story Empire State Building (1931) reaches 1,454 feet (443 m), while that of the 77-story Chrysler Building (1930) hits 1,046 feet (319 m). Yet as those skyscrapers rose to the sky symmetrically with Art Deco stylings, the asymmetrical, slablike tower designed by George Howe (1886–1955) and William Lescaze (1896–1969) brought International Style modernism to the American city.

Being considered International Style means following the three principles that curators Henry-Russell Hitchcock and Philip Johnson defined in their influential *International Exhibition of Modern Architecture* at the Museum of Modern Art in New York in 1932, a show that included the PSFS Building alongside primarily European buildings by the likes of Le Corbusier, Walter Gropius, and Ludwig Mies van der Rohe. First is a preference for volume over mass; second is striving for regularity over symmetry; and third is the avoidance of applied ornament. PSFS clearly meets these, though it does so incidentally, since Howe and Lescaze's design is the result of fulfilling practical concerns rather than expressing a specific style.

At the base, the ground floor was given over to shops to increase the middle-class area's street life; above was the banking hall, reached by escalators from Market Street on the north. Around the corner to the east on Twelfth Street was the entrance to the office core, which formed a T-shaped slab with the narrow rental office plates cantilevered subtly over the Market Street sidewalk. A full-floor truss above the bank lobby transferred the office slab's four rows of columns to two rows, giving the bank and shops open spaces. Each functional element was expressed in a modern whole, including the air-conditioning incorporated throughout (it was the second tall building in the United States to have AC when tenants moved into the building in August 1932). This last piece led to a sizable mechanical penthouse, which Howe and Lescaze treated with the same aplomb as the rest of the building, angling the eastern wall and mounting large PSFS letters in neon, an installation that remains to this day, even though the bank lost ownership of the building in 1992.

Although the structure was designed so carefully and exquisitely as a bank and office tower, the generous spaces of the base and the narrow slab above made its transformation into a hotel relatively simple. Since 2000 the landmark PSFS Building has served as the Loews Philadelphia Hotel, which, beyond the neon sign, has preserved the interior's lush finishes and the bank's vault, now a fixture in the hotel lobby.

1933 HAUS SCHMINKE

Hans Scharoun ▸ **Löbau, Germany**

A common path for practicing architects is to start with residential commissions and then move progressively toward larger and more complex projects. German architect Hans Scharoun (1893–1972) was no different, but the progression was less fluid, due to a break that came with the rise of the Nazis in 1933 and World War II. Once the war ended, Scharoun jumped immediately to much-needed large-scale housing, eventually realizing a number of theaters and concert halls, including the Berliner Philharmonie (1963), often considered his masterpiece. Haus Schminke, in eastern Germany near the Czech border, is the last—and best—of his modern houses before the war, a masterpiece of modern residential architecture on par with Villa Savoye (see 1931), Villa Tugendhat (see 1930), and Villa Mairea (see 1939).

Scharoun's client was Fritz Schminke, who followed his father as head of noodle manufacturer Loeser & Richter, and his wife, Charlotte. The site for the house was a sizable plot of land immediately next to the factory. Balancing solar orientation and proximity to the factory on the south with distant vistas and the garden on the north, Scharoun developed a linear, dumbbell plan oriented east-west along the site's slope. At the western end of the ground floor he positioned the kitchen and other service functions, while at the eastern end—closest to the road—he placed a conservatory with glass walls on three sides; in between was the open-plan living space, featuring built-in and movable furniture.

Variation from a straightforward, orthogonal plan came from the nearly 30-degree angle of the road on the east and the property line on the west. Scharoun angled the ends of the building as well as the interior stair and a double-height extension to the living space. It is done to particularly great effect at the conservatory where angled terraces, roofs, and an exterior stair congeal into a dramatic prow. The boat metaphor is reinforced by porthole openings in the roof and terrace, and circular patterns in the ceilings and glass walls inside.

The Schminkes and their four children moved into the house in 1933 but lived there for only twelve years, since the Red Army took control of it in 1945. Although they regained control of the house the following year it never served its original purpose again, instead becoming a community center for children under various associations. The house underwent a much-needed restoration in 2000, and since 2006 it has been run by the Schminke House Foundation, which offers visitors the opportunity to sleep in this modern masterpiece.

1934 ISOKON, LAWN ROAD FLATS

Wells Coates ▸ London, England

The building's prow seen from the south. World War II–era tenant Agatha Christie referred to the building as "a giant liner without any funnels."

Often recognized for its most famous occupant, Agatha Christie, who lived there from 1940 to 1946, the Isokon building is also referred to as the Lawn Road Flats. Other well-known, war-era tenants included Walter Gropius, Marcel Breuer, and László Moholy-Nagy. The building is significant as well for its modern, streamlined form, executed in reinforced concrete—the first time the material was applied to housing in Great Britain.

The project is the result of clients Jack and Molly Pritchard and their architect Wells Coates (1895–1958). Together they envisioned a block of "serviced flats" for young professionals, fitted out with the Pritchard's line of bent plywood Isokon furniture. Each unit was designed with a combined living room/bedroom, kitchenette, bathroom, and dressing room. Meals, shoe cleaning, and window washing were part of the building's "very full domestic service," as one advertisement stated at the time of the building's 1934 completion. In combination with its communal facilities—the Isobar restaurant designed by Marcel Breuer, laundry facilities, and a roof garden—the building was distinctively modern in function, not just appearance.

The four-story building faces east onto Lawn Road, not far from Hampstead Heath. The building is a dramatic departure from its context of brick row houses both in its aesthetic and siting. Reinforced concrete gives the building a monolithic appearance, aided by rounded corners and walkways that emphasize the horizontal. Given its narrow, tapered lot, the L-shaped building is set at an angle to Lawn Road, which results in a triangular forecourt and a dramatic prow where the stair meets the street at the southern tip.

After World War II, lack of maintenance and a concomitant deterioration plagued the building as it switched hands from the Pritchards to the *New Statesman* magazine in 1969, then to the Camden London Borough Council just three years later. A competition to restore the building, granted Grade One status in 2000, was won by a team led by the Notting Hill Home Ownership Association and Avanti Architects, with a proposal to maintain the thirty-four units in their original layouts, setting aside twenty-five units for public sector employees, and the rest as market-rate units. Faced not only with material and service deterioration and disrepair, but also a 1950s exterior stucco job and the unfortunate replacement of the original steel windows with ill-matched aluminum substitutes, the team had to overhaul just about every surface to bring back its original, Christie-era luster.

1935 DE LA WARR PAVILION

Erich Mendelsohn and Serge Chermayeff ▸ Bexhill-on-Sea, England

As most of the preceding buildings in this book attest, modern architecture at the beginning of the twentieth century was a European affair, home to the architects, schools, and clients supporting explorations in new forms and technologies. Yet with Adolf Hitler's rise to power, practitioners of Modernism fled first from Germany, and then from other countries affected by the conflict. One of those architects was Erich Mendelsohn (1887–1953), known first for Einsteinturm (see 1921), and then later, department stores utilizing extensive walls of glass. In 1930, the Jewish architect reached out to Serge Chermayeff (1900–1996), an architect based in London, for assistance, resulting in a professional partnership in 1933. Even though Mendelsohn & Chermayeff would last only three years, their De La Warr Pavilion is one of the first International Style buildings in Britain, one of the first welded (not riveted) steel structures anywhere, and an influential building in the design of seaside architecture.

The same year that Hitler came to power and Mendelsohn emigrated, the mayor of Bexhill-on-Sea, the Ninth Earl of De La Warr, persuaded the town to hold a competition for a new entertainment hall. Unlike earlier, Victorian-era structures in towns strung along England's Channel coast (aquariums, piers, zoos, and the like), the pavilion at Bexhill would be a high-class affair, such that even a modern aesthetic was called for explicitly in the competition brief.

Mendelsohn & Chermayeff's winning design proposed two rectilinear volumes—a narrow, two-story bar for the lounge, restaurant with dance floor, and reading room, and a wide, three-story bar for the auditorium—placed parallel to the shoreline and connected to each other by a hall and an elegant sweeping staircase. This last piece takes on a cylindrical form projecting from the otherwise flat south facade, like a pinwheel in the middle of the plan (it is echoed by the rounded north stair next to the drop-off and entrance). Terraces wrap the stair and the rest of this glassy elevation facing the water. One critic at the official opening on December 12, 1935, compared the building to "standing on the deck of a liner at sea."

De La Warr Pavilion was damaged and subsequently repaired after a barrage of German bombs hit the seaside town on September 30, 1941, but in the ensuing decades a combination of neglect and insensitive modifications left the building in a sorry state. Then in the 1980s the building was granted a Grade One listing, which paved the way for a lengthy restoration, headed by architect John McAslan, that returned everything from its facades to its modern interior fittings and furnishings to an immaculate state. Since 2005 the building has served as an arts center and community center while still carrying its original name.

1936 CASA DEL FASCIO

Giuseppe Terragni ▸ **Como, Italy**

West elevation. Terragni was persuaded to allow porcelain enameled photo panels on the marble wall of the facade overlooking the piazza, but thankfully they were never executed.

All architecture is political. At the simplest level, architects must navigate laws that dictate, to varying degrees, life safety, bulk, height, and sometimes even the appearance a building takes. On a deeper level, the buildings that architects design serve those in power, be they governments or corporations, whomever is able to employ an architect and construct a building. Buildings for the state are therefore the most overtly political ones, and none is more exceptional for its combination of art and politics in a modern vein than the Fascist Party (PNF) headquarters, called the Casa del Fascio (House of Fascism).

In a climate of political dissatisfaction in Italy following the Great War, Benito Mussolini and his Fascist Party rose steadily to power in the 1920s, taking hold of the parliament in 1926. Although vocal on most matters, the totalitarian leader was mute regarding architecture, which led some architects practicing Neoclassical architecture to come to the fore. In response to this reactionary trend, combined with the Beaux-Arts education prevalent in Politecnico di Milano and other architecture schools, seven architects, including Giuseppe Terragni (1904–1943), formed Gruppo 7 with "Rationalism" as their defining position. Their first physical realization was Terragni's Novocomum apartment building in his native Como. Its unadorned walls, large windows, and asymmetrical massing capably expressed Rationalism's logic and its interpretation of the spirit of Italian tradition. Novocomum was completed in 1929 around the time Terragni's brother became mayor of Como, an appointment that led directly to the architect's Casa del Fascio commission.

Terragni spent four years on the project—a quarter of his short working life—starting in 1932 when his brother arranged for a site behind the cathedral for a building combining meeting rooms, assembly areas, and offices for the PNF. Capturing the spirit of traditional Italian palazzi, the blocky Casa del Fascio was designed with a courtyard at its center, but Terragni enclosed it with a glass-block ceiling rather than leave it exposed to the elements. This central space is subtly expressed on the gridded and layered front facade through three open bays on the fourth floor and glass walls at the ground floor that provide access to the building. Once in the central hall, the residents of Como would have been able to see into the PNF meeting hall upstairs through more glass walls (the building is now home to Guardia di Finanza, the tax enforcement agency), an expression of the party's supposed political transparency.

1937 TALIESIN WEST

Frank Lloyd Wright ▸ Scottsdale, Arizona, United States

Drafting studio seen from the pool to the south. The low buildings are rooted in the desert landscape, heightened by the "desert masonry" below the translucent roofs.

Warm climates are known to exude a siren call toward people of retirement age, particularly those with the means to move there. In the United States, these places include the Sun Belt region, the southern states stretching from Arizona and Texas to Florida, with some of the greatest population growth in the last half-century. Frank Lloyd Wright (1867–1959), who lived in chilly Wisconsin most of his life, called the desert of the American West his "spiritual cathartic." In 1937, at the age of seventy, the great architect purchased some land outside of Scottsdale, Arizona, and established Taliesin West, the warm weather companion to Taliesin in Spring Green, Wisconsin. Like that Wright-designed complex, Taliesin West would be his home, but also the setting for his office and Taliesin Fellowship.

In the years before the establishment of Taliesin West, Wright worked in the desert on two separate hotel commissions. In 1929, he built Ocatillo, a temporary structure consisting of canvas stretched over wood framing for his draftsmen. Wright liked the effect of the light shining through the canvas; when it came time to design the buildings at Taliesin West he followed a similar approach, from the wood framing painted his signature "Cherokee Red" to the translucent ceiling that gave an even light to the larger spaces. One difference was the walls, made out of what Wright called "desert masonry," created by placing boulders and stones in wood formwork, filling the gaps with concrete, and removing the forms once the concrete hardened. These walls integrated Taliesin West more fully into its desert surroundings.

Wright began by designing and building his office, the drafting room, apartments, and the Kiva, a small theater for the performances that were so important for the fellowship, due in large part to Wright's third wife, Olgivanna, who incorporated her dance background into her life at Taliesin. While these first structures were completed by 1940, Wright added and renovated buildings, such as the striking Cabaret Theater that replaced the smaller Kiva, until his death in 1959, the same year the Guggenheim Museum (see 1959) opened in New York. The differences between the spiraling Guggenheim and Taliesin West make it clear how Wright's extraordinary creativity stemmed from context. The qualities of Taliesin West's two-decade long design arose from the desert landscape: in the way the buildings reach across the land, in the way movement between the various structures orients to the surroundings, and in the way windows frame views of natural landmarks such as Maricopa Hill.

1938 FALLINGWATER

Frank Lloyd Wright ▸ Mill Run, Pennsylvania, United States

Fallingwater seen from the south. A clearing in the trees offers a picture-postcard view of the house perched over the waterfall on three concrete piers evident below the lowest terrace.

As legend has it, the most famous house of the twentieth century was drawn by sixty-eight-year-old Frank Lloyd Wright (1867–1959) on September 22, 1935, in the time it took his client, Pittsburgh department-store magnate Edgar Kaufmann, to drive west from Milwaukee, Wisconsin, to Taliesin in Spring Green, Wisconsin, a distance of only 120 miles (193 km). While the exact details of when Wright started sketching the house are unknown, it is clear he had the design in mind for a good nine months after he first visited the site. And what he put on paper that September day turned out to be a remarkably precise representation of what would be built three years later.

More amazing than the storied speed with which Wright drew the plans was that he proposed to place the country house for the Kaufmann family directly above a 20-foot-tall (6 m) waterfall on their property in Western Pennsylvania. Instead of a house located on the south with a view toward a stream on the north, as Kaufmann had anticipated, Wright placed the house on a rock ledge on the north edge of the stream, fusing house and waterfall. What is still shocking decades later must have been all the more so for Kaufmann, who relished the bold idea and moved forward with the daring design. Executed at around the same time as Wright was hired by Johnson Wax to design its Administration Building (see 1950) in Racine, Wisconsin, both projects push cantilevered concrete construction to its limits.

Fallingwater is a three-story house that rises from stone walls wedded to the site and three parallel concrete piers that support the main volume of the house over the waterfall. The main floor houses the living room (and its famous boulder hearth), kitchen, two terraces, and a hatch to the level of the water below. Each of the two smaller bedroom floors above is set back from the floor below, resulting in even more terraces. It is a highly complex massing whose image is simplified through horizontal and vertical elements; the former as solid concrete parapets at the terraces, the latter as stone walls rising to the house's apex.

The Kaufmanns moved into an incomplete Fallingwater in 1937. It was completed the following year, and the family occupied the house until 1963, when it was entrusted to the Western Pennsylvania Conservancy, which maintains the house and operates tours to this day. Deflection of the concrete cantilevers led to the erection of temporary supports in the late 1990s, but major repair work was carried out in 2002 to correct the deflections and exhibit Wright's masterpiece as it must have appeared in his mind's eye back in 1935.

1939 VILLA MAIREA

Alvar Aalto ▸ Noormarkku, Finland

South view. Many of the villa's well-known details were provoked by the artistic Maire, who the house is justifiably named after and who set up the Maire Foundation, which hosts guided tours of the house.

As with Frank Lloyd Wright's Fallingwater (see 1938) in the woods of Western Pennsylvania, Alvar Aalto's (1898–1976) Villa Mairea is wedded to its natural site. Yet whereas Wright's house is aptly positioned directly over a waterfall, Aalto's villa is situated in a clearing in the pine forests of Western Finland. Although Aalto was inspired by Wright's house, which was famous even while under construction— he went so far as to encourage his clients to build over a stream—Villa Mairea is a microcosm of the wooded site it merges into. It is also a pivotal design in the oeuvre of one of the twentieth century's most original architects.

In 1933 Alvar and his wife, Aino, moved to Helsinki. Two years later they met Maire Gullichsen (née Ahlström), and along with Nils-Gustav Hahl, founded Artek in order to sell Aalto's furniture and glassware, which the company continues to do to this day. The Ahlström family owned a giant timber and wood-pulp company, and Maire's husband, Harry, headed its board of directors. As an avowed modernist he was instrumental in involving Aalto in designing the company's projects, such as a cellulose factory and workers' housing in Sunila in Southern Finland. It was only natural that the Gullichsens had Aalto design a country house for them and their children, the third house built on Ahlström land in Noormarkku and the first in the modern vein.

After Aalto abandoned the attempt at creating a Finnish Fallingwater, he designed the L-shaped "Proto-Mairea" that the clients approved but which Aalto modified even after the foundation was poured and the house was completed in 1939. Eventually the house became U-shaped in plan, oriented to the west. The open living space and master bedroom are stacked on the south; the kitchen and servant quarters sit below the children's and guest bedrooms on the east; and the sauna, connected to the house by a covered walkway but not completed until 1946, is located on the north adjacent to a pea-shaped pool.

The massing and materials of the house are collagelike, an intertwining of contemporary purist themes with the Finnish Karelian vernacular: whitewashed surfaces punctuated by projecting windows; Maire's undulating, timber-clad studio jutting beyond the footprint of the living room below; and a generous free-form canopy signaling the entrance at the meeting of the two main wings of the house. Slender wood posts bundled together support this last piece, an allusion to the forest beyond, echoed in the famous wrapped columns of the living space, the timber poles screening the main stair, and other treelike supports both inside and outside. Like the forest space around the villa, the space inside the house, particularly the living area, flows around the columns and screens. Ultimately Villa Mairea's collage of forms and forestlike space crystallizes into a whole where no single part takes precedence over the other, just like the nature that inspired it.

1940 SKOGSKYRKOGÅRDEN

Erik Gunnar Asplund and Sigurd Lewerentz ▸ Enskede, Sweden

The Woodland Chapel. Carl Mille's *Angel of Death* sculpture marks the entrance to the chapel Asplund completed in 1920.

The Crematorium. Seen through the portico, from right to left: the path leading from the cemetery entrance, Asplund's Granite Cross, and the Grove of Remembrance across the pond.

The few buildings at Skogskyrkogården in southern Stockholm are insignificant relative to the landscape. Faced with a 124 acre (50 hectare) tree-covered site, Erik Gunnar Asplund (1885–1940) and Sigurd Lewerentz (1885–1975) let the landscape dictate much of their 1915 competition-winning design. Rather than impose strong axes across the site, they laid out paths that freely followed its contours, allowing most of the buildings to reveal themselves as people moved across the landscape. Their submission was chosen for its harmony between the built and the natural, and more than one hundred years later it is considered a masterpiece of spiritual architecture and landscape.

Asplund and Lewerentz decided to team up for competition in 1914. With space needed in Enskede since at least 1905, and debates in Sweden having carried on about cremation versus burial for much longer, a crematorium would become an integral, and highly visible, component of Skogskyrkogården, though not until 1940, the same year of Asplund's untimely death. The competition program asked for easy orientation arising from a clear layout and extensive vistas on the site, and in their revised scheme of 1916 they addressed concerns that there were too many trees by including clearings that balance the dense sections of forest.

Although the architects worked closely together on the larger plan until 1935, for the most part individual buildings were the purview of one or the other. Lewerentz notably designed the main entrance (1931) and the Neoclassical Chapel of the Resurrection (1925), while Asplund was responsible for the Service Building (1924) that now serves as the Visitor Center, the Woodland Chapel (1922), and the Crematorium (1940). These last two are particularly commendable given their pared-down designs that balance indoor and outdoor space. The small chapel integrates itself into the surrounding trees with its large-scaled hip roof over a portico and a surprising domed space inside. The austere Crematorium and its three chapels are the most overtly visible buildings in the cemetery, particularly the great portico with its stone square columns, which strikes a balance with the Grove of Remembrance across the clearing.

Lewerentz would carry out work until 1961 primarily on the landscape design, but the most recent major addition to the cemetery since 1940 came with the 2013 completion of a new crematorium designed by Johan Celsing. Like Asplund's Woodland Chapel, the new building is cut into the forest and discovered as one walks the paths of the spiritual landscape.

1941 NATIONAL AND UNIVERSITY LIBRARY

Jože Plečnik ▸ **Ljubljana, Slovenia**

Gosposka Street elevation on the east. The reading room is visible on the left side of the brick-and-stone facade, expressed by the tall window bisected by a mock-Ionic column.

Facing three streets on nearly a full block steps away from the Ljubljanica River, the National and University Library is one of numerous buildings, landscapes, and pieces of infrastructure Jože Plečnik (1872–1957) designed and renovated in Ljubljana after he returned to the city from Vienna and Prague in 1920. Just two years before his return, the former Austro-Hungarian Empire was christened the Kingdom of Serbs, Croats, and Slovenes, with Ljubljana named the capital of the new Slovenia. As a result, Plečnik's architecture between the wars strove to instill a newfound national pride, most overtly in the library he began designing in 1930.

The National and University Library, which traces its history back to 1774, moved into its new building in 1941 on the site of the seventeenth-century Prince's Mansion (destroyed by an earthquake in 1895). Although a fairly cramped and confined location, the library is given some relief on Vegova Street to the west, where it is set back from the street like its neighbors to the north and south. At the southern terminus of Vegova Street, just beyond the library, is a market and monument also designed by Plečnick, while just past the northern end of the street at Zvezda Park is his famous Triple Bridge that connects the historic and modern parts of the city on either side of the Ljubljanica River. Another Plečnik pedestrian bridge, the Cobbler's Bridge, spans the river near the northeast corner of the National and University Library. It's no wonder that the city is often called "Plečnik's Ljubljanica."

The plan of the library is a trapezoid—*almost* a perfect square—that follows the shape of the historic medieval streets. At its center is a courtyard pierced by a stair lined with local Popdeč marble. This stair cuts the courtyard into two smaller spaces and connects the entrance on the north (Turjaška Street) with the double-height reading room on the south. A raised, south-facing window in the reading room combines with a transom over the door to illuminate the stair and symbolically elevate the importance of the Slovenian literature housed in the library. More light comes into the reading room through large, double-layer windows on the east and west elevations that are punctuated by fluted, mock-Ionic columns on the outside, a detail that made Plečnick appealing to postmodern architects four decades later. The rest of the building is covered predominantly in orange brick with small windows and speckled with a variety of local stones and concrete set into the brick, giving the library its distinctive appearance—an unprecedented yet adroit expression of the building's purpose as a storehouse of history.

1942 CRANBROOK ACADEMY OF ART

Eliel Saarinen ▸ Bloomfield Hills, Michigan, United States

The Cranbrook Art Museum seen from the south. The large Triton Pool that sits on axis with the building's peristyle contains just a few of the many Carl Milles sculptures dotting Cranbrook's campus.

Not long after the completion of the Helsinki Central Railway Station (see 1919) and placing second in the Chicago Tribune Tower competition of 1922, Finnish architect Eliel Saarinen (1873–1950) embarked for the United States. But homesick with only teaching jobs coming his way, he and his wife were ready to return to Finland only two years later. Thankfully, that same year he was asked to develop a plan for what would become the Cranbrook Academy of Art, a masterpiece of modern American campus architecture that followed the Arts and Crafts tradition, and whose pedagogy was based on the artist-in-residence program at the American Academy in Rome.

Although Saarinen came on board in 1925, Cranbrook dates back to 1904, when George and Ellen Booth bought an old farm outside of Detroit as a summer home for themselves. Over time they decided to add community facilities such as the Meeting House in 1918; it eventually expanded to become the Brookside School, one of six distinct institutions set on Cranbrook's 319 acres (129 hectares). Saarinen was responsible for many of the buildings and complexes created over the course of nearly two decades: the School for Boys (1929), the Kingswood School for Girls (1931), an addition to the Institute of Science (1938), and the Academy of Art, which included the Saarinen Residence (1930) and the Academy Art Museum, which was completed in 1942 and concluded Saarinen's architectural work at Cranbrook (he served as director of the Academy of Art from 1932 until 1946).

Saarinen's design for the Academy of Art consists of one building split into two parts—a library and a museum—that are connected in the basement and by a generous peristyle. This raised colonnaded space frames a north-south axis with linear pools and numerous sculptures by Swedish-born artist Carl Milles. Another opening at the end of the museum's east wing aligns with the east-west axis formed by the gardens of the Booths' main house designed by Albert Kahn, just one example of how the landscape has continually influenced the campus's architecture (the Natatorium that alumnus Tod Williams designed with his partner Billie Tsien subtly yet gracefully terminates that axis on the west). Inside Saarinen's understated design in brick and stone are generously scaled and carefully illuminated gallery spaces, a reading room, and an auditorium.

Within the past twenty years, Cranbrook has expanded with an addition to the Institute of Science (1998) designed by Steven Holl, the aforementioned Natatorium (1999), and at the Academy of Art two additions to the east of the museum: the Studio Building (2002) designed by Rafael Moneo, and the Collection Building (2011) designed by SmithGroupJJR, which also renovated the museum.

1943 MINISTRY OF EDUCATION AND HEALTH

Le Corbusier and Lúcio Costa ▸ Rio de Janeiro, Brazil

Le Corbusier (1887–1965) made two major trips to Rio de Janeiro between the two world wars: in 1929 he sketched his famous urban plan for the city, and in 1936 he devoted much of his time to a layout of the University of Brazil. During the latter trip he was approached by a relatively young Lúcio Costa (1902–1998) to consult on the design of the Ministry of Education and Health in Rio's central area. The Swiss-French architect agreed and the resulting design became the first expression of modern architecture in the country, a fusion of European modernism and local considerations.

Although the impetus for the ministry project was Brazilian president Getúlio Vargas, who mandated it as part of his Estado Novo (New State) program, its modern direction can be attributed to the Minister of Education, Gustavo Capanema. Finding the entries to the architectural competition for the complex not modern and progressive enough, Capanema hired Costa, who developed an initial scheme, but then approached Le Corbusier to oversee the project. Le Corbusier proposed a piece of land closer to the water and ditched Costa's U-shaped courtyard in lieu of a cruciform plan. Before he returned to his Paris atelier, he sketched an alternate design for the original site with a tower raised on *pilotis* accompanied by two low volumes, close to the final result.

After Le Corbusier's departure, Costa worked with fellow Brazilian architects Affonso Eduardo Reidy, Carlos Leão, Jorge Moreira, and Ernani Vasconcelos to adjust the latest design. (In one of his first projects, Oscar Niemeyer worked as an unpaid intern in Costa's office.) They moved the tower so it had some breathing space from its neighbor, increased the height of the *pilotis*, and widened the portico under the tower, among other changes. As built, the main building is a fourteen-story office tower that sits above and perpendicular to a two-story building with an auditorium, exhibition hall, and a rooftop garden designed by Roberto Burle Marx. The tower has north and south exposures, and the former is shielded from the sun by a gridded facade of vertical concrete piers fitted with operable horizontal louvers. This last feature gives the project its signature expression of International Style modernism adapted to Brazil's climate and culture.

Although Le Corbusier was not entirely happy with handing the project over to Costa and his colleagues, he nevertheless grudgingly agreed to do one more sketch, one that showed the building in its finished state. Although this gave the impression that Le Corbusier was the driving force behind the design, history has shown that Costa and company were greatly responsible for the design's success, and therefore, to a degree, the subsequent spread of Modernism throughout the region.

North facade of tower block. This insertion of European modernism into South America is tempered by local climate, most overtly in the deep north facade with movable horizontal louvers.

1944 SOLIMAR BUILDING

Manuel Copado ▸ Havana, Cuba

Seen along Calle Soledad from the south. The eight-story building's wavy, wraparound terraces, inspired by the waters of the nearby bay, stand out from the older buildings in central Havana.

Modern architecture in Cuba is a much different beast than in other countries, Americas or otherwise, partly due to the country's history, but also because of the mid-twentieth-century turmoil and revolution that limited modernity's influence. After gaining independence from centuries of colonial rule (and a brief US military occupation) in 1902, Cuba became a test bed of sorts in eclectic, typically revivalist styles of architecture: Art Nouveau, Renaissance, Neocolonial, and a brief but impressionable stint with Art Deco. Yet from the mid-1920s until 1965 and the start of Communist rule, Cuba, and Havana in particular, saw an abundance of International Style modernism, most of it in residential architecture. Architectural historian Eduardo Luis Rodríguez splits these forty years of modern architecture into two phases: an early phase from the mid-1920s until the mid-1940s, followed by a mature phase that lasted until 1965; the former is defined by pared down, rational designs, while the latter buildings are more sculptural, as evidenced by the unfinished National Art Schools that the unsympathetic Communist government closed in 1965.

On the rough dividing line between these two phases is the Solimar Building, an eight-story apartment building in central Havana designed by Manuel Copado. The combination of the ornament-free concrete exterior and the undulating form of the balconies facing Calle Soledad give the building an appearance that bridges the rational and the sculptural. The novel form of the building is in clear opposition to the colonial architecture that surrounds it, but the name Solimar, which translates to "sun and sea," clearly signals the inspiration: Copado's wavelike design is only two blocks from the waters of the Caribbean. More than an image, the balconies give the residents views toward the water while ensuring privacy from people making their way along the busy street and shading the interiors from the sun. Further, the building has a narrow footprint that spans one full block, so each flow-through unit has the benefit of natural ventilation.

In hindsight, the building appears like a merger of Frank Lloyd Wright's Fallingwater (see 1938) and the Aqua Tower (see 2009) by Jeanne Gang. Fallingwater's concrete terraces may have been a precedent for Copado, and I like to think that the wavy form of Solimar fits into a lineage—that includes the residential towers of Harry Seidler, among others—of buildings finding inspiration in the ever-changing movement of water. With diplomatic relations between Cuba and the United States restored, it is a likeness that many more people can determine in person.

1945 CASA DEL PUENTE

Amancio Williams ▸ **Mar del Plata, Argentina**

The house seen from the northwest. The parabolic form of the arch mirrors the banks of the stream below.

Just as Frank Lloyd Wright opted to build a weekend house (Fallingwater, see 1938) for Edgar Kaufmann over the site's defining water feature, Amancio Williams (1913–1989) designed and built a house for his father over a stream. Similarities between the two houses end there, for Wright's house is structurally and formally idiosyncratic, while Williams's house is rational and modern.

Commissioned by his father, a well-known composer, soon after the younger Williams graduated from the School of Architecture at the University of Buenos Aires in 1941, Casa del Puente (House over the Brook, or Bridge House) is situated on a 5-acre (2-hectare) lot. The house proper is a rectangular plan, 30 feet (9 m) wide by 90 feet (27 m) long, resting on hollow concrete columns at either end, where the entrances to the raised interior are found. Stairs follow the main structure, an arched, reinforced concrete slab that spans the creek and supports a series of thin transverse walls below the floor of the house. The stairs rise to face each other in the middle of the house. From here, facing the northern sun, the living space wraps around to the west by the kitchen. Most of the southern half of the plan is given over to three bedrooms that receive sunlight through north-facing skylights above the closets. The closets and other service elements (fireplaces, kitchen cabinets) are arrayed along the center longitudinal axis of the house, incorporating concrete walls that support the accessible concrete roof. The structural independence of floor and roof results in a continuous band of windows that wraps around all four sides of the house above the concrete sill.

Gazing out through these windows, the viewer feels immersed within the surrounding trees, as if floating in space. The latter sensation arises from being lifted twice the distance above the surface of the water. In its form, the house capably bridges the two sides of the property while giving people a unique perspective upon it, as if to fuse the house into its context.

Following the elder Williams's death, the house was used as a radio station, but it was abandoned in the early 1990s and then subject to vandalism. In 2004 a fire destroyed the interior, leading to concern for the house's future. The municipality of Mar del Plata purchased the house in 2012, put in some new windows and opened it to the public in 2013, but more work needs to be done to rejuvenate this modern residential masterpiece.

1946 DYMAXION DWELLING MACHINE

R. Buckminster Fuller ▸ Dearborn, Michigan, United States

Inside the open living space. The view may be trompe l'oeil, but it gives an accurate sense of how the windows were designed to be truly panoramic.

The building inside the Henry T. Ford Museum. Visitors ascend a ramp to reach the interior of the dwelling that is elevated on its central mast.

Richard Buckminster "Bucky" Fuller (1895–1983) designed the Dymaxion House in 1927, but it was not realized until immediately after World War II, when he coined it the Dymaxion Dwelling Machine. (An adman came up with the distinctive name by following Fuller around for a few days and combining some of the words he heard the engineer-designer drop: dynamic, maximum, and tension.) The earlier version, designed for Marshall Field's department store in Chicago, was technically and financially decades ahead of its time; so was the later version, as Fuller's ideas have yet to take hold.

Whereas the original Dymaxion House had a hexagonal floor plan, its cantilevered construction off a central mast was carried through to the circular Dymaxion Dwelling Machine. Inspired by the automobile industry, Fuller envisioned the aluminum dwelling as the residential equivalent of cars: mass-produced, relatively lightweight and inexpensive, and spatially efficient at only 1,100 square feet (100 sq. m). Air ducts, piping, bathrooms, and utilities occupied the center of the 36 foot (11 m) diameter building that was lifted above the ground on its central column and capped by a rotating rudder-vent designed to draw stale air from the interior. A panorama of windows circled the whole 360-degree plan, while "wedges" of space were given over to an open living area, kitchen, and two bedrooms. Modular storage units radiating from the center served as partial-height partitions between the different rooms.

Only one version of the Dymaxion Dwelling Machine was built, in Wichita, Kansas: rather than close the B-29 Superfortress bomber factories there at the end of the war, the house was seen as a promising peacetime use of the factory and its employees; and given that the house was designed to resist even tornadoes, southern Kansas was an ideal spot to put the house to the test. The Wichita House, as it was familiarly called, was built in 1946 and even though some positive postwar buzz accompanied news of the house's mass production, work on the Dymaxion Dwelling Machine halted the same year, due to disgruntled stockholders, tooling costs, and Fuller's stubborn assertion that the design just wasn't ready for mass production.

Abandoned after the owner died, the Wichita House was bought in 1991 by the Henry T. Ford Museum, which disassembled the house, cleaned and restored its 3,000 components, and rebuilt it inside the museum in Dearborn, Michigan. Today it is on display as a piece of history, as something that could have been; but it is also an inspiration for designers wishing to take Bucky's ideas ahead into the twenty-first century.

1947 PAMPULHA

Oscar Niemeyer ▸ **Belo Horizonte, Brazil**

Saint Francis of Assisi church. The street elevation of Pampulha's sole religious building is a wonderful integration of sculptural concrete forms and expressive *azulejo* artwork.

Museo de Arte da Pampulha. The former casino is made up of a rectangular volume (right) and a curving volume, the latter overlooking the artificial lake at the center of Pampulha.

Architectural histories tend to recognize three decisive moments in modern Brazilian architecture: the completion of the Ministry of Education and Health (1943) in Rio de Janeiro, the creation of the country's new capital in Brasília (1960), and the four buildings at Pampulha designed by Oscar Niemeyer—each of these projects has Niemeyer's involvement in common. The buildings he realized at Pampulha broke new ground in terms of architectural expression, opening up the country's architects to free forms that departed from orthodox modernism. Niemeyer would go on to a long career marked by striking, often curvilinear forms, most notably at Brasília and the MAC (1996) in Rio de Janeiro, but it's safe to say none of those buildings would have been possible without his liberating work at Pampulha.

The man who made this happen was Juscelino Kubitschek, then mayor of Belo Horizonte. He dreamed of a lakefront settlement accompanied by a casino, church, dance club, hotel (unbuilt), and sailing club (Kubitschek also hired Niemeyer to renovate his house in Belo Horizonte, and when he became president of Brazil, he turned once again to Niemeyer for Brasília). All parts of the project were wrapped up by 1947, but the first building completed, in 1942, was the two-story casino, sited on a promontory overlooking the artificial lake. It was designed as an orthogonal volume when seen from the car drop off, and from across the water, a rounded volume lifted above the steep slope on *pilotis*. (Its days as a casino were short-lived, since gambling was declared illegal in 1946, but since 1957 the building has served as a museum.) Next came the yacht club, a two-story rectangular volume with generous terraces on the top floor, followed by the dance club, a circular space joined by a curling walkway canopy.

While these three buildings have concrete, transparency, formal plasticity, and Roberto Burle Marx landscapes in common, it is the Saint Francis of Assisi church that breaks the most ground in terms of architectural expression and structural innovation. A large parabolic arch caps the nave of the church, but from the street—the back of the altar—the building appears as a series of smaller wavelike arches. This nautical metaphor is reinforced by artist Candido Portinari's blue-on-white *azulejo*—a traditional ceramic tile surface made fresh again in Le Corbusier's Ministry of Education and Health (see 1943)—that covers the whole wall below the arches. In its depiction of scenes from the life of St. Francis across a geometric background, the wall is an artistic masterpiece whose integration into the architecture points to another influential contribution coming out of Pampulha.

1948 CASA LUIS BARRAGÁN

Luis Barragán ▸ **Mexico City, Mexico**

The garden from the living space. The cross-shaped framing of the glass wall lends religious overtones to the view of the lush garden.

In conferring the second Pritzker Architecture Prize on Mexican architect Luis Barragán (1902–1988) in 1980, the jury commended "his commitment to architecture as a sublime act of the poetic imagination." He realized these poetic acts through numerous houses and gardens, but also a chapel and stables in and around Mexico City, where he worked from 1936 until his death. Each project consisted of a strong garden component, such that Barragán considered himself a landscape architect and saw gardens as necessary places of beauty and spirituality. His own house on Calle General Francisco Ramírez in Mexico City's Tacubaya section expresses the poetry and beauty of his architecture in the most personal of ways.

Before he moved into this house in 1948, Barragán lived in a neighboring house and garden where he experimented with the creation of living spaces from existing structures. Like that building, his house sits behind an unassuming street facade, primarily a blank wall with a few square windows and three doors (a garage door, a door to the house, and a door to the architect's studio). A white tower and orange wall projecting above the roofline hint that something special is found through these doors. Those who make an appointment to visit the house, which is now run as a museum, enter a narrow corridor with steps ascending to an entry vestibule gaining light from above. From here three options are available: turn left to ascend to the bedrooms upstairs; walk forward toward the kitchen and dining area; or veer right into the living spaces. In all cases the rooms are oriented to the garden, the walled-off landscape invisible from the street. Most dramatic is the living space, one large double-height space that is broken down by partial-height walls and varying floor heights. One entire wall is a large window with cross-shaped framing that looks onto the garden, a perfect place for daydreaming.

Throughout the interior, color is of the utmost importance, as it was for all Barragán projects. Everything, from the color of the tile to the paint on the walls, the wood beams and floors, the paintings on the walls, and the trees through the windows, was considered for effect, most overtly in terms of beauty. The colors are nowhere more pronounced than on the roof terrace, where the sun illuminates walls of white, red, and earthy brown. Cut off from the house and garden below, the roof terrace is one with the sky, a place of contemplation much different from the intimate spaces below, but at the same time following Barragán's unique and personal sense of design.

1949 GLASS HOUSE

Philip Johnson ▸ **New Canaan, Connecticut, United States**

The Glass House on approach from the southeast. Only the brick cylinder housing the bathroom and fireplaces pierces the otherwise open space of the glass box.

Even with a concerted attempt not to feature overly similar buildings in this book's selections, it is difficult to not include both the Glass House by Philip Johnson (1906–2005) and Ludwig Mies van der Rohe's Farnsworth House (see 1951). Yet what appear to be almost duplicate designs—glass-and-steel boxes with open plans designed for individuals on large properties—are highly dissimilar, arising from different clients, sites, and architects. One characteristic that sets apart Johnson's Glass House from just about any residential project of the twentieth century is that it is one of many buildings that Johnson built on his New Canaan estate, each reflecting the trends of their respective times.

Johnson took a circuitous route to building the Glass House. Educated in history and philosophy at Harvard University, he founded the Architecture and Design Department at the Museum of Modern Art (MoMA) in New York in 1932, and mounted its influential *International Exhibition of Modern Architecture* the same year. Johnson returned to Harvard in 1940 to attend architecture school, when he built his Thesis House on a lot in Cambridge, Massachusetts; primarily solid on three sides, the one-story house featured a full-height glass wall on the fourth side facing an enclosed yard. A few years after graduation he purchased 5 acres (2 hectares) of land in New Canaan, Connecticut, a one-hour train ride north of New York City, almost immediately finding the ideal location for what would become the Glass House. It wasn't until 1947 when he saw Ludwig Mies van der Rohe's sketch for the Farnsworth House that he had an inkling of what exactly to build there, transforming the selective transparency of the Thesis House into a four-sided wrapper open to the surrounding landscape two years later.

Visitors to the now 47-acre (19-hectare) property—owned since Johnson's death by the National Trust for Historic Preservation, which conducts tours in warm months—approach the Glass House after passing his Deconstructivist Da Monsta (1993) and catching glimpses of other follylike additions, including the Brick House also built in 1949. Framed with eight steel columns, the 1,720 square-foot (160 sq. m) Glass House sits squarely on its patch of land protruding into an escarpment at the back of the original five acres. Fixed and movable elements within the house—the cylindrical brick bathroom and fireplace, the kitchen, the wardrobe, the artworks, and the furniture—define intimate spaces within the otherwise open plan. Likewise, the various buildings added to the site from the 1960s to the 1980s create spaces within the landscape that Johnson and longtime companion David Whitney cultivated for five decades.

1950 JOHNSON WAX BUILDINGS

Frank Lloyd Wright ▸ Racine, Wisconsin, United States

Fortaleza Hall and Research Tower. The tower's alternating full and mezzanine floors are apparent in this view from next to Norman Foster's addition to SC Johnson's Racine office campus.

Administration Building work space. Wright designed the chairs and desks to complement his rounded architecture, and SC Johnson has maintained some of them in the work space.

While it may be trite, there is truth in the statement that behind every great building is a great client. For Frank Lloyd Wright (1867–1959), perhaps his greatest client was Herbert F. Johnson, the third-generation head of SC Johnson, known as Johnson Wax for much of its existence. Not only did Johnson shelve an uninspired design in favor of hiring Wright for the company's Administration Building in 1936, he hired Wright again to design the Research Tower, even though the former building suffered from leaks and the two personalities had a love-hate relationship due to, among other things, spiraling costs. But with innovation at the core of both SC Johnson's company philosophy and Wright's architecture, client supported architect so the latter could create one of the greatest buildings—and building complexes—of the past one hundred years.

Architectural historian Kenneth Frampton has stated that Wright's buildings tended to veer from the introverted to the extroverted; the former often commercial and urban, the latter rural and residential. Of the four Wright buildings in this book, two of them are rural and open themselves up to their surrounding landscapes— Taliesein West (see 1937) and Fallingwater (see 1938)—while the two urban projects (Johnson Wax and the Guggenheim Museum [see 1959]) close themselves off from the city around them. This opposition stems from Wright's appreciation of nature and outspoken dislike of cities, especially Racine. In turn, nature was the model for the introverted Administration Building, completed in 1939: the grand, half-acre ($1/5$-hectare) work space is a tall, forestlike space formed by what Wright called lily-pad columns. Between the petals he placed tubes of Pyrex glass (the source of the leaks until a proper sealant was found decades later) that bathed the space in an aqueous light and made the analogy with lily pads appropriate.

The following decade, Wright proposed a 15-story tower for the research facilities, a vertical counterpoint to the horizontal, streamlined volume of the Administration Building. Wright wrapped the Research Tower on all four sides with the same Pyrex glass and brick found in the first building, making an aesthetic connection between the two buildings but also cutting off views of surrounding Racine from inside the tower. Yet with stacks of two-story spaces formed by alternating full and mezzanine cantilevered floors, and only a single tiny stair in its amoebalike core, the tower was only in use from 1950 to 1982.

Following a yearlong restoration that ended in 2014, the company opened the partially used Research Tower to the public as part of its weekend tours, when visitors can also take in the Administration Building, which remains in use.

1951 FARNSWORTH HOUSE

Ludwig Mies van der Rohe ▸ Plano, Illinois, United States

The house's elevation facing the Fox River. The approach gives the house an asymmetrical composition, where the steps lead to an intermediate plane and an open porch with a side entry into the house.

Although Philip Johnson completed his Glass House in 1949, having seen a sketch for the Farnsworth House in 1947, he admitted the influence of the house Ludwig Mies van der Rohe (1886–1969) finished two years later for Dr. Edith Farnsworth. The similarities between the domestic one-room, glass-and-steel boxes are obvious, but the differences are evident mostly in how the houses sit upon the land, how they express their steel structures, and how they influenced the architects' future work. Simply put, Johnson's Glass House rests on the landscape, its black steel structure is integrated with the glass framing, and the modern design fits within a stylistically diverse output; Mies's Farnsworth House is lifted above the landscape, its white steel structure is overtly expressed, and the house exists within a continuum in his quest to create "almost nothing." Differences aside, the floor-to-ceiling glass walls in each house frame their landscapes as images to be appreciated from within.

Mies gained the commission after meeting Farnsworth at a dinner party in 1945; she knew of the architect and wanted him to design a weekend house for her 9-acre (3.5-hectare) property next to the Fox River southwest of Chicago. Given the river's tendency to overflow its banks each spring, he placed the floor of the house just over 5 feet (1.5 m) above the ground to let the water flow under it. Even with such measures, floods in 1996 and 2008 necessitated the creation of "Barnsworth" by architecture students from the Illinois Institute of Technology (which Mies headed from 1938 until 1958) to protect and exhibit the house's wooden wardrobe.

With the need to elevate the house, steel was the logical choice for the structure, particularly given Mies's explorations at the time for achieving a "universal space" with long-span structures. The steel columns seem to magically hold up the floor and roof of the 1,400 square-foot (130 sq. m) house—welded joints do the trick. Even though the once intimate relationship between architect and client soured over time, leading to two lawsuits, Farnsworth said she liked the idea of her house as a prototype for a new American architecture.

In 1972, after using the house for twenty-one years, Farnsworth sold it to Peter Palumbo, who removed the screens Farnsworth added to the porch (done, like the wardrobe she requested, to the architect's specifications) and made extensive changes to the grounds. He auctioned off the house in 2003, when Landmarks Illinois and the National Trust for Historic Preservation managed to buy it, saving it from being moved and, like the Glass House, opening it up for public tours.

1952 SÄYNÄTSALO TOWN HALL

Alvar Aalto ▸ Säynätsalo, Finland

The town hall's east elevation. The democratic importance of the government building is accentuated by the council chamber, which rises above the rest of the two-story brick building.

Alvar Aalto's (1898–1976) entry in the invited competition for the Säynätsalo Town Hall in 1949 was titled "Curia" (the place where the senate met in ancient Rome). In 1925 Aalto had honeymooned in Italy with his first wife, Aino (who died in 1949), and he would do so again in 1952 with his second wife, Elissa. These trips, and the references embedded within the name of his competition entry, signal the lasting Mediterranean influence on the Finnish architect, evident in the winning design, a castlelike mass surrounding a courtyard atop a hill—an Italian cityscape in miniature realized on an island in the center of Finland.

Then as now, Säynätsalo is home to only a few thousand people, but the wood factories run by Enso-Gutzeit (now Stora Enso) made it an appropriate location for an ambitious town hall with even more ambitious architecture. In addition to offices and a council chamber for the municipal government, the project included a community library, apartments for staff, and shops. Aalto's plan put the functions into a two-story square courtyard building that is cut by two exterior stairs leading to the raised open space and the building's main entrance. The architect justified the elevated courtyard technically as fill created from the excavation of the building foundations, but it also resulted in a two-way, internal-external orientation for the two floors: the lower floor backs up against the fill and therefore looks out to the surrounding town and landscape (an appropriate place for the shops, for example), while the upper floor faces out onto the contained nature of the courtyard. Further, when seen from a distance the brick building has a commanding presence, but from the courtyard the building has a small, even domestic scale that recalls the Villa Mairea (see 1939).

The main departure from the two-story plan is the council chamber, which rises in a stepped, cantilevered brick mass in its spot next to the east exterior stair, the formal entrance to the town hall (the west exterior stair is less formal but more famous, made from sod compacted into wood forms). The height of the chamber is accentuated by the pitched roof that is supported on the inside by fan-shaped trusses, one of the few Aalto flourishes that departs from the load-bearing brick that predominates.

Over time, many of the nonmunicipal spaces were converted to offices. Since 1993 the municipality of Säynätsalo has been part of the city of Jyväskylä, but the building still serves much of its intended purpose. Even the apartments that were renovated into office space have been turned back into apartments, making this one of the few Aalto buildings that "architourists" can spend the night in.

1953 CIUDAD UNIVERSITARIA DE CARACAS

Carlos Raúl Villanueva ▸ **Caracas, Venezuela**

Aula Magna Hall. Alexander Calder's *Flying Saucers* turn an unremarkable auditorium into a room-sized work of art.

Plaza Cubierta. The covered plaza is an open space that tempers Caracas's tropical climate through concrete roofs and breezeblock walls.

Following the end of World War II, two Latin American countries realized major "city" universities that, in addition to utopian tendencies and new forms of modern architecture, shared a strong integration of art and architecture. In Mexico City, architect Mario Pani, with architecture students Enrique Molinar, Armando Franco, and Teodoro González de León, designed the Universidad Nacional Autónoma de México (UNAM) campus in an axial arrangement with primarily blocky buildings, highlighted by the library covered in a colorful mosaic by Juan O'Gorman. In Venezuela, Beaux-Arts-trained architect Carlos Raúl Villanueva (1900–1975) laid out the smaller 500-acre (200-hectare) Ciudad Universitaria de Caracas (part of the Universidad Central de Venezuela, UCV), designed more than forty of its buildings, and involved artists to create interior and exterior environments based on pedestrian movement. Although the UNAM was also completed in 1953, the UCV is featured here because of the diversity of art incorporated into its buildings and because it is a grand assemblage of one architect, something echoed more than a half-century later in Wang Shu's Xiangshan Campus for the China Academy of Art (see 2013).

The UCV campus is shaped like an east-west oriented ellipse, with the University Hospital on the east and sports facilities on the west; construction began with the former in 1945 and exhibits Villanueva's classical architecture training in an axial arrangement of buildings and symmetrical plans, while the latter includes some of his most daring modern architecture rendered in concrete. Of interest here is what lies between those ends—the Central Area, the administrative and cultural heart of the campus. Villanueva composed the buildings, paths, and art contributions into five movements like a musical score, meandering from the entrance court and museum on the north to the concert hall and library on the south. Murals, sculptures, and screens by Jean Arp, Fernand Léger, Mateo Manaure, and Victor Vasarely, among numerous Venezuelan and European artists, dot the "movements," a path accentuated by the covered walkways rendered in concrete (engineered by Otaola and Benedetti). But the highlight of the myriad syntheses of art and architecture is found in Aula Magna Hall, the largest of sixteen auditoriums on campus, where Alexander Calder's acoustic *Flying Saucers* turn the sweeping but otherwise unexceptional space into something dreamlike—alien, as the title indicates, but unmistakably Calder.

Beyond the skill in merging art into the buildings and landscapes of UCV, Villanueva should be commended for his modern interpretation of open, ventilated architecture. The covered walkways shelter students and faculty from the sun or the rain, and porous concrete block walls—aptly named breezeblock—facilitate airflow, important for the school's tropical location.

1954 MILL OWNERS' ASSOCIATION BUILDING

Le Corbusier ▸ Ahmedabad, India

West elevation. As if to accentuate the importance of the Jain industrialists, the long ramp leads to the floor where the president and other executives had their offices.

Understandably, Chandigarh (1965) is the most famous project that Le Corbusier (1887–1965) realized in India. Working with his cousin Pierre Jeanneret (Le Corbusier was born Charles-Édouard Jeanneret-Gris) in the early 1950s, he laid out a master plan for the administrative capital of the state of Punjab in the recently independent India, while also designing a handful of buildings and even furniture. Though the buildings have been admired for their sculpted concrete exteriors with deep-set facades, the urban planning of the complex has received, like Brasília, criticism for its ignorance of the pedestrian scale. Yet as he began work on Chandigarh, Le Corbusier also ventured to Ahmedabad, the largest city in the western state of Gujarat, and ultimately designed five buildings (four were realized) for the city's wealthy Jain industrialists. A highlight of these is the former Mill Owners' Association Building, now the offices of the Ahmedabad Textile Mills' Association (ATMA).

Located on the west bank of the Sabarmati River, the four-story cubic building shares numerous traits with the larger Chandigarh buildings: exposed concrete, deep facades integrating brise-soleil, and open spaces for natural ventilation. Le Corbusier made the north and south side walls solid brick and concentrated his efforts on the porous east and west facades. The street and therefore main approach is from the west, via a long ramp (foreshadowing the Carpenter Center of the Visual Arts, 1963) that delivers people one story up into the middle of the building. On either side of the covered, triple-height entrance hall are angled concrete walls— brise-soleil—that cut down considerably on the afternoon sunlight that hits the building. The east side of the building, facing the river, features shallower, orthogonal brise-soleil that, while not as effective as the west side in terms of providing shade, offer expansive views of the river where the wealthy owners could see the heart of their business: workers washing and drying clothes among the birds, cows, and donkeys.

Vertically, the building was originally separated into two zones, both functionally and climatically. The lower two floors contained offices enclosed by glass walls behind the concrete facades. The top half of the four-story building functioned as a semi-cultural venue, with an oval, double-height auditorium that popped above the roof on one side and a mezzanine bar with roof access on the other side. Outside of the enclosed auditorium, these two floors were open to the elements, so while the bottom floors worked well in terms of shade, ventilation, and protection from rain, the top half the building suffered from its openness, unable to provide protection from the seasonal monsoons. Regardless of this deficiency, the monumentality of the edifice effectively expressed the economic and political importance of the textile industry in Ahmedabad, just as the buildings in Chandigarh expressed the nation's independence.

1955 NOTRE DAME DU HAUT

Le Corbusier ▸ Ronchamp, France

Interior view from pulpit. Le Corbusier hand-painted the glass in the small openings of the south wall with flowers, words ("Marie"), faces, birds, and other imagery.

View from the southeast. Le Corbusier designed the small chapel to be understood from the pilgrimage route, with the south wall on the west leading to the entrance and the east wall on the right used for outdoor services.

If any architect popularized the notion that modern architects go through phases of artistic evolution, it was Le Corbusier (1887–1965). His first buildings in vaguely historical garb gave way to the famous Purist houses, which articulated his famous Five Points of Architecture (see Villa Savoye, 1931). Following that highly influential phase, he abandoned the whitewashed expression in favor of heavy structures of exposed concrete with deep-set windows. The most idiosyncratic building in this last phase is the small pilgrimage chapel he designed for the Œuvre Notre Dame du Haut on a hilltop site in eastern France.

The Chapel at Ronchamp, as it is often called, is the most sculptural of Le Corbusier's buildings. Its unanticipated form led critics to grasp for metaphors (steamship, duck, cupped hands), but the architect, who first visited the site in 1950, called the commission "totally free architecture." Nevertheless, an intentional metaphor is found in the dark, thickened roof, inspired by a crab shell the architect found years before on a Long Island beach. As built, the roof is hollow, made of two concrete skins held apart by beams, constructed much like a ship's hull or an airplane wing. The beams rest on concrete columns that are embedded within battered walls of stone rubble, their surfaces finished in stucco and painted white. The main walls are oriented to the pilgrimage approach from the southeast: the south wall, with a random smattering of small openings, is splayed out to draw people to the chapel's entrance, while the recessed east wall, with an altar and pulpit, is the backdrop for outdoor services, such as the one on June 25, 1955, when the building was consecrated.

The sculptural decisions on the outside make sense when seen from the inside, though the results are just as unexpected. While the roof and walls appear solid from the outside, on the inside, the former appears to float above the latter on a narrow gap filled by glass. The three towers that pop above the roof—one visible on approach and two on the north elevation—correspond with side chapels that are bathed in colored light from above. The dark, cavelike main space, sloping toward the altar, receives much of its character from the southern wall. Here, the random openings, small on the exterior, flare out to larger interior dimensions.

Details like the floating roof and openings that look alternately small and large sound like an architecture of deception, but the spatial effect is transcendental and understandably one of the most prized works of twentieth-century architecture.

1956 S. R. CROWN HALL

Ludwig Mies van der Rohe ▸ Chicago, Illinois, United States

Main entrance on the south. Crown Hall fits into Ludwig Mies van der Rohe's lineage of clear-span structures, evident in the deep girders spanning across the single open space.

In 1938, the Illinois Institute of Technology (IIT), founded in the late 1800s as the Armour Institute of Technology, invited Ludwig Mies van der Rohe (1886–1969) to chair its architecture department and design the master plan for a new campus. Working with six blocks deemed as blighted and slated for clearance on Chicago's South Side, Mies ordered the superblock tabula rasa into a 24 square-foot (7.3 sq. m) grid. This module was suited to individual classrooms as well as to offices and laboratories in fractions and multiples, respectively, but it was also used to position the more than twenty campus buildings and therefore shape the spaces in between them.

By 1954, when construction finally began on a building for the architecture school on the site of the fabled Mecca apartment building, the module had shifted to twenty feet. Although the difference seems minor (twenty and twenty-four are multiples of four, after all), S. R. Crown Hall is architecturally distinct from Mies's previous IIT buildings, so the departure makes sense. Gone are the infill brick walls between steel columns that prevailed in the primarily two-story buildings; in their place are all-glass walls wrapping what is in effect one space 220 feet (67 m) wide and 120 feet (36.5 m) deep. The most dramatic difference is the roof structure: four six-foot (1.8 m) deep girders span the full width of the building to suspend the roof, create the unbroken open space and effectively mark the southern edge of campus.

Mies is attributed with the famous saying, "God is in the details," and those at Crown Hall are telling. Entry to the building on the south is via steps and a large porch, both reminiscent of the Farnsworth House (see 1951), a definite precursor to this larger clear-span structure. The glass wall at the entrance is clear, but elsewhere the lower panes are translucent with clear glass above, a detail that echoes the use of brick for privacy on the earlier IIT buildings.

As the last ingredient in Mies's IIT master plan, carefully restored in 2005, S. R. Crown Hall continues to influence architects with its distinctive approach to Modernism. Since 2003, after decades of Mies's campus sitting sacrosanct, IIT added contemporary buildings to the modern mix—a student center designed by Rem Koolhaas, a dormitory designed by Helmut Jahn. Now local architect John Ronan is adding an "Innovation Hub" north of Crown Hall.

1957 MILLER HOUSE AND GARDEN

Eero Saarinen ▸ Columbus, Indiana, United States

Interior with conversation pit. Eero Saarinen said he came up with the idea of the conversation pit in the 1940s, and although they became a cliché in the 1960s, there is no finer example than the one in the Miller House.

View from the southeast. The house sits at the north end of the property, buffered from the neighbors by trees and hedges.

Modern architecture came to Columbus, Indiana, in 1942, with the First Christian Church designed by Eliel Saarinen. During the following decade, his son Eero Saarinen (1910–1961) would add three buildings to the town located just southeast of Indianapolis: the Irwin Union Bank and Trust Company (1954), the North Christian Church (1964), and this house, for the man primarily responsible for bringing a historic collection of modern architecture to the middle of America's heartland.

In 1934, J. Irwin Miller began working at the firm founded by his great uncle, Cummins Engine Company (now Cummins), a manufacturer of diesel engines. Though only in his twenties at the time, Miller turned the fortunes of the business around and eventually became its president and then chairman. In the 1950s he created the Cummins Engine Foundation Architectural Program, in which the company would pay architectural fees for new schools and other public buildings, under the stipulation that distinguished national architects would be hired. In due course, Columbus became an architectural mecca featuring buildings by Saarinen, as well as Edward Larrabee Barnes, Gunnar Birkerts, César Pelli, Victor Gruen, Charles Gwathmey, Richard Meier, I. M. Pei, Kevin Roche (an employee of Saarinen who worked on the house), Robert Venturi and Denise Scott Brown, and Harry Weese.

Since 2014, three years after the death of Miller's wife, the impressive list of buildings to visit in Columbus has included the Miller House and Garden, now owned and operated by the Indianapolis Museum of Art. Before it opened to the public, it was an unknown masterpiece of modern American residential architecture (owing to the Millers' privacy).

A collaborative effort and a work of art where one contribution did not overshadow the others, Saarinen's design for the rectangular one-story house exploits the steel structure with deep overhangs on all sides and a grid of skylights following the flowing, cruciform-shaped living space in the middle of the plan. The white marble walls, travertine floors, and white plaster ceiling of the living space is offset by the furnishings and fabrics of Alexander Girard (1907–1993), most notably in a custom storage wall beneath one of the skylights and the sunken conversation pit that respects the openness and asymmetry of the space. Landscape architect Dan Kiley (1912–2004) picked up on the geometric rigor and flowing spaces of Saarinen's design by creating outdoor "rooms" defined by rows of honey locust trees and saucer magnolias, and perpendicular "walls" of carefully trimmed hedges. For about fifty years the integration of house and landscape was a grand setting for the Millers and their five children, but now it is one that anybody visiting Columbus can appreciate.

1958 SEAGRAM BUILDING

Ludwig Mies van der Rohe ▸ New York City, United States

The west facade seen from Fifty-Third Street and Park Avenue. Mies's meticulous control of details extended to the window blinds, which can be fully open, fully drawn, or half drawn.

Just as Le Corbusier has been unfairly blamed for the ills of postwar, "tower-in-the-park" urban renewal, the onus for bland glass boxes in downtowns across the United States and elsewhere has fallen onto the legacy of Ludwig Mies van der Rohe (1886–1969). Mies spent the last two decades of his life focused almost entirely on high rises in urban cores, producing subtle variations on the glass box articulated with nonstructural I-beam mullions. He also excelled at creating plazas that wed his buildings to their urban contexts, which he perfected with the Seagram Building in Midtown Manhattan, such that the plaza facing Park Avenue, the 39-story tower behind it, and the McKim, Mead & White building across the avenue were fused into one urban assemblage.

Mies's involvement in the project is due almost entirely to Phyllis Lambert, daughter of Samuel Bronfman, then head of Seagram. In 1954, when she was pursuing art in Paris, Bronfman sent her a rendering of the tower he wished to build. She wired her reply with a string of "No"s and promptly returned home. After a three-month search for an architect, Mies was chosen and Lambert became director of planning for the company's headquarters. They were joined by Philip Johnson, who worked on the interiors, the plaza, the fountains, the lighting, and the Four Seasons Restaurant, where he was a staple until his death in 2005.

The tower occupies approximately half of the site, though what looks like a rectangular prism is actually made up of three volumes: the main block facing Park Avenue to the west, a narrower section rising the same height on the east, and a wider four-story bustle also on the east where the Four Seasons is found. This massing enabled the flat, abstract elevation that faces the plaza, a facade that gains presence through its generous setback, bronze framing, bronze tinted glass, and the perimeter lighting on the office floors designed with Richard Kelly.

Beyond putting his own building on display, Mies's setback tower also gives prominence to Charles McKim's Racquet and Tennis Club directly across from it. Here, his appreciation of classical architecture comes to the fore, as the two symmetrical buildings are linked together across the space of the plaza. Just as Mies's towers spawned inferior imitations by architects who didn't understand the basis for his designs, New York and other cities incorporated plazas that do not give to the city nearly as much as Seagram does. It is a lesson that still needs to be learned.

1959 SOLOMON R. GUGGENHEIM MUSEUM

Frank Lloyd Wright ▸ New York City, United States

Interior view. The circular space of the atrium in the middle of the spiraling ramp is skillfully violated by a convex bump-out around the service core.

View from the west. The highly controversial early-1990s addition by Charles Gwathmey is a quiet backdrop to Wright's coiling drum and its appendages.

Before the Guggenheim, as it is known, opened across from New York's Central Park in October 1959, just about all museums deferred to the art on display, with a series of galleries stacked behind typically Neoclassical facades. After the Guggenheim—its galleries descending down a ramp curling around an atrium—museums had another option: they could make architectural statements and force the art to bend to their will. This "new" approach is visible to lesser degrees in the Guggenheim Museum Bilbao (see 1997) in Spain as well as MAXXI (see 2010) in Rome, a kind of unfurled Guggenheim. Of course, art museums aren't relegated to this simple either/or condition, so a number of recent ones merge fairly traditional galleries with Guggenheim-inspired flourishes, be they atria and ramps (Iberê Camargo Foundation, see 2008) or attention-getting wrappers (The Broad, see 2015). It is impossible to imagine the design of these and other museums in the past fifty years without the influence of Frank Lloyd Wright's (1867–1959) final building.

In June 1943, Wright received the commission from Solomon R. Guggenheim and his art adviser Hilla Rebay to design a home for their collection of nonobjective paintings, and in his first drawings early the following year he already had the basic design of what would be built—fifteen years later! Wright envisioned visitors ascending an elevator to the top floor, right below the rotunda's glass dome, and then descending along the unfurled ramp with the galleries set into perimeter alcoves under skylights; the angled walls, much bemoaned by curators after 1959, were present in the beginning and meant to evoke painters' easels. Museumgoers would be able to see across the atrium to other galleries, and upon arrival at the bottom they would take in the entirety of the space under the dome, an artwork in and of itself. Although the glass skylight was covered upon completion, the renovation and addition carried out by Charles Gwathmey's firm in the early 1990s reglazed it, bringing it closer to Wright's original intention.

The Guggenheim can be seen as the culmination of Wright's exploration of organic architecture and freely flowing space, but it is also the realization of his desire to build a spiraling, nautilus-shaped building—a dream that had been waiting for the right client, location, and technology. The last occurred with concrete that was sprayed or "gunned" rather than poured, then sanded and painted to its final appearance. Over time cracks appeared on the exterior, necessitating a major restoration that took place from 2004 to 2008, completed just in time for the building's semicentennial.

1960 CHURCH OF CHRIST OBRERO

Eladio Dieste ▸ **Atlántida, Uruguay**

Interior. The low, curved wall of the altar screens off the chapel and sacristy behind it.

Church front facing north. The thinness and solidity of the brick walls and roof are evident in the sections that extend past the front wall.

Until he gained the commission in 1952 for the Church of Christ Obrero (Church of Christ the Worker), Eladio Dieste (1917–2000) was considered an engineer, not an architect. He spent the first decades of his career running calculations for large warehouses with long-span brick vaults. Approached by a donor wanting to build the church at minimal cost, Dieste recommended hiring an architect, but the donor believed the poor community of workers employed at the resort town of Atlántida wouldn't require anything with architectural merit. Dieste took the job and agreed it would not cost more than one of his warehouses, but in exchange he wanted total design control. Eight years later Dieste finished what is considered his first architectural commission, a poetic construction of undulating brick walls and roof.

In essence what Dieste delivered was a warehouse: a single space—approximately 50 feet wide, 100 feet long, and 25 feet high (15 × 30 × 7.5 m)—defined by a brick floor, brick walls, and a brick roof. A plan cut just above floor height actually would resemble a squared-off rectangle, while one cut just below the roof would reveal two sine waves at the side walls. These conoidal walls alternately lean in and out to give the just one-foot-thick (30 cm) brick walls reinforced with steel wires increased structural capacity; the double-curvature vaults of the roof are reinforced by tie-rods hidden in the edges that project beyond the walls. As if to accentuate the shape of the walls and roof, as well as the way the two elements meet, Dieste recessed the entrance so that the brick surfaces project beyond the front wall, a gesture that invites people into the church.

The otherwise solid interior receives daylight through small openings in the undulating walls that are filled with colored glass and onyx, perhaps influenced by Le Corbusier's Notre Dame du Haut (see 1955). Dieste carefully positioned the openings so that they point toward the altar rather than into the eyes of parishioners. More light enters the church from louvered brick walls fitted with operable onyx panels at the top of the front wall, as well as gaps at the edge that make it appear like the front wall is freestanding. At the opposite end of the space, a partial-height brick wall wraps behind the altar; its shape recalls the "open-arm" plan of Bernini's colonnade at St. Peter's, but for Dieste, the idea was to bring the congregation and priest together in one space fusing innovative structural engineering and architectural poetry, echoing the mandates of the Second Vatican Council that would follow in a couple of years.

1961 SAINT JOHN'S ABBEY CHURCH

Marcel Breuer ▸ Collegeville, Minnesota, United States

View from the east. While the sizable trapezoidal bell banner propped upon four legs at the front of the church attracts much attention, the sides are highlighted by triangular pleated concrete facades.

A traditional mainstay of Catholic churches has been the carillon, housed inside a tower to call congregants to prayer and give the church a presence within the townscape. Even in modern churches that influenced or responded to the reformations of the Second Vatican Council in the 1960s, the bell tower remained. Surely one of the most unique examples is the "bell banner" that fronts the church Marcel Breuer (1902–1981) designed for the Benedictine monks of Saint John's Abbey.

Founded in 1863 on approximately 2,000 acres (810 hectares) of land northwest of St. Cloud, Minnesota, the abbey sits between three lakes (East Gemini Lake, Lake Sagatagan, and Stump Lake). The usual approach to the abbey is via Interstate 94 a few miles to the north. From here the 112-foot-tall (34 m) bell banner is visible above the trees. It also stands as the visual terminus of the main north-south drive on the campus that consists of numerous other Breuer buildings. Yet when he unveiled the design of the tower with the rest of the church in 1954, it was the element criticized the most. Like any architect, Breuer had modified the design through numerous iterations, but in the end the trapezoidal shape of the bell banner remained, a shape that hinted at the sacred space beyond it.

Before Breuer unveiled his initial design, he explored five shapes for the overall plan, from a traditional cross to the eventual trapezoid. Upon its consecration on August 24, 1961, the shape of the single space reflected the new liturgical principles being addressed by the Second Vatican Council. The plan gives more room at the back for the congregation and tapers toward the front where the choir is located. The altar sits in between, highlighted by a lantern cut into the concrete roof and a high altar suspended in space. The trapezoidal shapes of the plan and the bell banner are also reiterated in the north wall, structured by concrete, hexagonal windows with stained glass designed by Bronislaw Bak. It's the folded plates of the concrete walls and roof, engineered by Pier Luigi Nervi, that give the sacred space cohesion and lend credence to the argument, first articulated by Auguste Perret with Notre Dame du Raincy (see 1923), that concrete is a suitable material for buildings of faith.

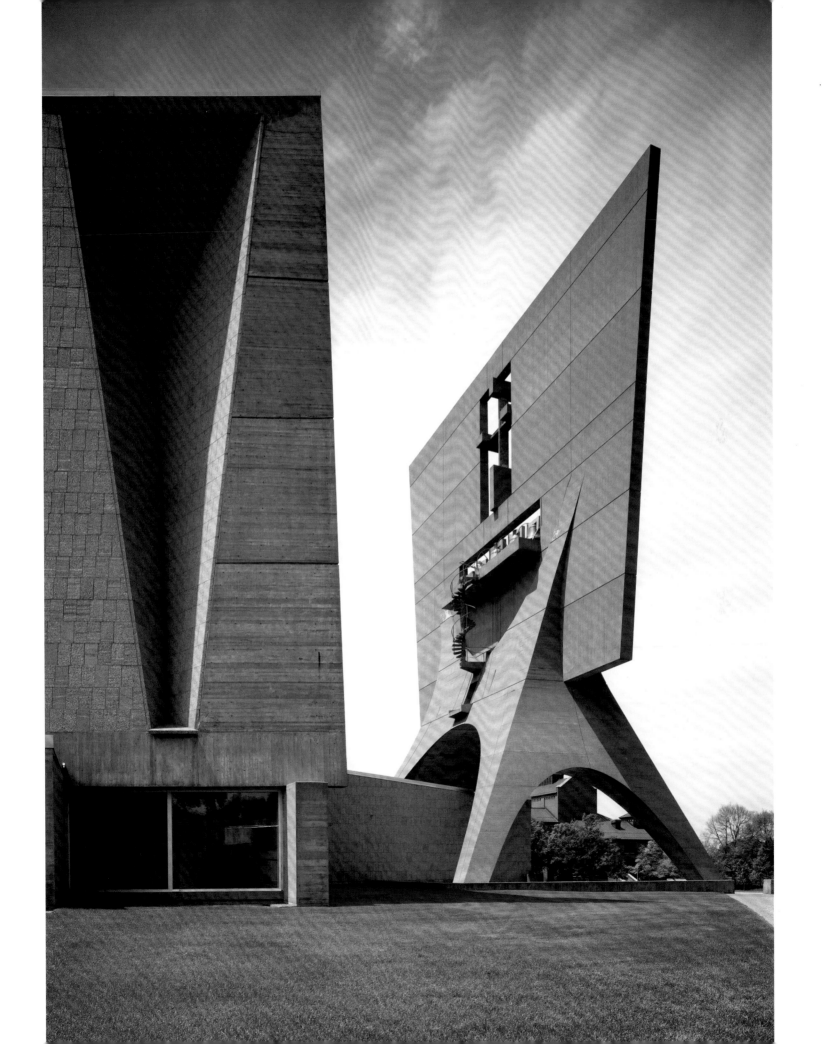

1962 NORDIC PAVILION

Sverre Fehn ▸ Venice, Italy

Interior. Fehn left gaps in the grid of concrete beams to allow existing trees–the only verticals in the otherwise uninterrupted open space–to poke through.

Unlike the rest of Venice's glorious maze of canals, wall-to-wall buildings, and narrow walkways, the Giardini is a parklike green space that has hosted the Venice Biennale since 1895, and in alternating years since 1980, the Architecture Biennale. Scattered throughout the Giardini are thirty pavilions representing the cultural works of thirty participating nations. The pavilion for the Nordic countries— Finland, Norway, and Sweden—was created through a 1958 competition won by Sverre Fehn (1924–2009). Faced with a site between the United States and Danish pavilions dense with plane trees, the Norwegian architect took what might have been impediments and incorporated them into the design of the pavilion.

Fehn won the competition the same year he completed the Norwegian Pavilion at the Brussels World's Fair, and the two designs share an emphasis on substantial flat roofs lifted above primarily transparent walls. Yet, whereas the temporary pavilion in Brussels had a solid roof, the overlapping grids of perpendicular concrete beams in the permanent Venice pavilion allow the trees to rise through the porous overhead plane. The open floor space is made up simply of a solid slab of marble underfoot and horizontal beams overhead. The only verticals to accompany the trunks in the middle of the space are solid walls to the north and east, and a single column in the southwest corner that appears to hold up the whole roof. The largest of the existing trees used to sit by the column, so Fehn split the beam into a Y-shaped cantilever that wrapped the tree, yet another respectful gesture in the pavilion and one that recalls his later work at the Hedmarksmuseet (see 1974). Unfortunately the tree came down this century, but the gesture remains.

While the combination of sliding glass walls on the south and east sides, and the roof pierced by trees gives the impression that the pavilion is literally open, it is capped by wavelike translucent panels that channel rainwater toward the trees and admit a soft overhead light to the space. Fehn stated that he wanted to create a Nordic atmosphere with Mediterranean light, and the multifaceted roof construction diffuses the light entering the space from above to eliminate shadows and bathe whatever is on display in an even light.

Just outside the footprint of the pavilion, in its southeast corner, is an anomaly: a ziggurat stair that connects the low and high parts of the Giardini landscape. Yet the overly steep profile of the steps makes it appropriate for unplanned activities: sitting, eating, lecturing, and performing. And from the steps one gets a good look at the horizontal beams intersecting the vertical trees.

1963 YALE ART AND ARCHITECTURE BUILDING

Paul Rudolph ▸ New Haven, Connecticut, United States

The Visitor's Suite. In addition to the corduroy-like concrete walls and columns, the distinctly orange carpet ties the interior of the A&A Building together.

View from the southeast. The pinwheel plan culminates in the vertical towers rising in an asymmetrical disposition about the corner of Chapel and York Streets.

At the beginning of the twenty-first century, Paul Rudolph (1918–1997) was the poster child for Brutalism and the negative view of the short-lived trend of aggressive forms, rough concrete, and monumentality. Three houses he designed between 1959 and 1979 were demolished in 2007, two public schools designed within the same time frame were demolished in 2009 and 2013, and in 2015 partial demolition began on Rudolph's 1973 Orange County Government Center in Goshen, New York, despite numerous lawsuits and criticisms over the uninspired design that would replace much of it. Yet even as his neglected, damaged, and unloved buildings met the wrecking ball, there were signs of hope, due in part to a renewed appreciation of Brutalism and certain enlightened building owners, none more so than Yale University with its Art and Architecture Building designed by Rudolph.

Like Walter Gropius at the Bauhaus (see 1926) and Ludwig Mies van der Rohe at IIT (see 1956), Paul Rudolph was the head of the architecture school he began designing in 1958. Located across the street from Louis I. Kahn's Yale University Art Gallery (1954), the A&A Building, as it was known for most of its existence, was designed for expansion on the lot to the north. Rudolph's building was finally "completed" with the Loria Center addition designed by Charles Gwathmey in 2008, when the original building was renovated and christened Rudolph Hall. Yet for Rudolph, that expansion could have happened across the street via bridges, thanks to what he called the pinwheel motion of the upper floors, which was generated by the plan shaped like a #. Within the long arms of the pinwheel he placed classrooms, lounges, stairs, and bathrooms, but in the middle of the plan—as defined by four large, concrete columns—he placed, from the basement to the top of the building, a lecture hall, the library, a double-height exhibition hall, a sunken crit space for the architecture studios, and art studios.

Beyond the bush-hammered, corduroy-like concrete finish that is employed inside and out, the most remarkable aspect of Rudolph's design is the internal complexity of the section. Across nine stories (seven of them above-grade), there are an amazing thirty-seven changes in level and ceiling heights that range from 7 feet (2.1 m) to 28 feet (8.5 m). Easily the most dramatic spaces are devoted to the architecture studios, which traverse five levels around the double-height crit space. Unfortunately these spaces are off-limits to the public, though the exhibition and lecture hall are open to the public at appropriate times, a taste of the complexity Rudolph passed on to his and subsequent students through the example of the building.

1964 YOYOGI NATIONAL GYMNASIUM

Kenzō Tange ▸ **Tokyo, Japan**

The small stadium seen from the east. Although the stadium roofs recall traditional Japanese buildings, they are highly functional, utilizing a structural suspension system and bringing in natural light.

If there is one building type that evenly balances the creative contributions of architect and engineer, it is the stadium. The coming together of throngs of people in a sizable building with high visibility requires an architect to, more than usual, equally address functional and formal expression. This means the success of a stadium design relies to a high degree on the relationship between the architect and engineer, especially in how well they strengthen each other's contributions toward a building that works as well as it looks. In this regard, the pair of gymnasiums Kenzō Tange (1913–2005) designed with Yoshikatsu Tsuboi (1907–1990) for the 1964 Summer Olympics in Tokyo is one of the most successful collaborations of the two disciplines.

The Yoyogi National Gymnasium was not their first collaboration. In 1951 Tange hired Tsuboi to work on the Hiroshima Children's Museum, which featured a formally simple but structurally complex concrete shell roof. Subsequent projects, such as St. Mary's Cathedral (1964) in Tokyo, continued to explore the possibilities of concrete shells, but when it came time to design and build the Yoyogi National Gymnasium, concrete proved too costly, and an alternative needed to be pursued. The most obvious route was to exchange the compressive strength of concrete for the tensile strength of steel, a choice that led to the suspension system used for both stadiums: the 15,000-seat venue for swimming and diving, and the 4,000-seat venue for basketball and other indoor sports.

Two masts tied back to concrete anchors hold up the petal-shaped roofs of the larger building, while just one mast is needed to support the twisting roof of the smaller building. Tange rationalized the bridgelike suspension system for a few reasons: the concave section of the roof eliminated wasted space up high that would need to be conditioned in spaces with convex, arched roofs; the system created physically and psychologically open, column-free spaces for the crowds to move through; and the structure and forms would point to the future direction of modern architecture. The most remarkable moments happen where steel meets concrete: the band where the roof connects to the cantilevered seating tiers, and the way the roof is pulled back like a drape to admit entry to the spaces that will once again host the Olympics in 2020.

1965 SALK INSTITUTE

Louis I. Kahn ▸ San Diego, California, United States

Although Louis I. Kahn (1901–1974) worked intermittently in the two-and-a-half decades between his 1924 graduation from the University of Pennsylvania and his three-month stay at the American Academy in Rome in 1950, all that he built in that time has been overshadowed by his work from the last two-and-a-half decades of his life. Kahn ascribed the change from some fairly run-of-the-mill modern architecture to a style that was simultaneously personal and timeless to his stay at the academy, during which he explored ancient buildings in Italy as well as in Egypt and Greece. He returned from the months abroad with a newfound appreciation of mass, monumentality, and order, first expressed in the Yale University Art Gallery (1953). In this first decade back he gained the most attention with the Richards Medical Research Building (1960), which was under construction when Dr. Jonas Salk, inventor of the polio vaccine, visited Kahn at his Philadelphia office in 1959. Although the Richards building received harsh criticism from the scientists who used it, architects praised Kahn's clear expression of "served" and "servant" spaces. The following year Salk hired Kahn to design labs that even "Picasso could come to visit."

None of the functional criticism launched at the Richards building went toward the Salk Institute, probably because the client knew exactly what he wanted: large, open laboratories that could be set up flexibly and rearranged easily over time. Kahn complied with Salk's wishes and gave him large rectangular labs, but instead of separating served and servant in plan, as at Richards, he did so in section. The resulting six-story building is split into two mirrored halves across a plaza, linked on the lowest level, with three floors of labs (and three interstitial floors of "pipe space" to serve the respective lab spaces below). To one side of the labs, pushed toward the plaza, are four-story study towers (local codes placed a cap on the height of the building, so two of the six floors are below-grade), with their monastic cells for respite from the lab work. Angled walls with windows give the scientists in the studies views toward the Pacific Ocean, paralleling the view from the plaza below.

The plaza is one of the most iconic open spaces of the twentieth century, highlighted by a linear fountain pointing westward toward the ocean. The space is all travertine, concrete, teak, and sky, although Kahn initially envisioned it as a lush green space; a visit made by Mexican architect Luis Barragán during construction convinced architect and client to leave it empty. Instead of just a space between the buildings, the plaza is a space with direction, connected to the infinite beyond the cliffs, beach, and water.

1966 BANK OF LONDON AND SOUTH AMERICA

Clorindo Testa and SEPRA ▸ **Buenos Aires, Argentina**

View from the southwest. Although the concrete building stands out among the older buildings, the carved corner provides some relief in the dense streets.

In the 1960 competition brief for the Argentinian head office of the Bank of London and South America, the organizers asked for a clear and concise architectural statement free of both historical styles and fashionable trends. The winning design by Clorindo Testa (1923–2013), a painter and architect, with Santiago Sánchez Elía, Federico Peralta Ramos, and Alfredo Agostini of the architecture firm SEPRA, certainly delivers upon that request, placing a monumental concrete structure on a corner lot within the narrow streets of the downtown Buenos Aires banking district. The building's modern break with its neoclassical surroundings is accentuated by its proximity—only one block away—to Casa Rosada, the office of the president of Argentina, which sits in Plaza de Mayo, the city's oldest square.

In addition to a progressive design, the bank wanted the competing architects to design a flexible layout structured on a modular system. The winning design's standout appearance addresses these considerations through a simple *parti*: concrete floors float within a six-story glass box wrapped by a screen of repeated concrete piers facing the street. To create a flexible layout the architects split the building's total of nine floors roughly into thirds: the lower third is below-grade and houses the parking, vaults, and services; the middle third is devoted to the lobby, tellers, and other public areas, with its fairly small floors built like bridges supported by two concrete cores; while the upper third is devoted to private offices on floor plates hung from the sizable beams at the roof that are connected to the outboard piers. Each floor of the interior is held apart from the glass curtain walls that rise unimpeded from the sidewalk to the roof.

By placing the vertical structure on the exterior, in front of and independent of the curtain wall, considerations of interior flexibility and contemporary expression are united. Exuding the influence of Le Corbusier's late Brutalist phase, as found in buildings like the Unité d'habitation (1952) and the Convent of La Tourette (1960), the structure is expressed as deep and narrow concrete piers bundled into groups of six that are braced by lateral walls punctuated by rounded openings. These modules shade the interior and give the exterior a consistent rhythm, while framing views of the surrounding buildings for those inside. The only departure from this structural system happens at the corner, which is eroded to clearly indicate the entrance to what is now the Banco Hipotecario—the Bank of London and South America having closed in 1986, twenty years after the completion of this landmark of Argentinian and Latin American modern architecture.

1967 HABITAT 67

Moshe Safdie ▸ Montreal, Canada

Although the massing is symmetrical due to the load-bearing requirements of the modules, unexpected diagonal vistas occur through and across the spaces between them.

If such a thing as the zeitgeist exists in avant-garde architecture, in the 1960s it was the construction of megastructures: large-scale sections of the city built from smaller cells or modules. Archigram envisioned a Plug-in City in Britain; Kenzō Tange wanted to fill Tokyo Bay with a string of Metabolist structures; and Paul Rudolph proposed a chain of stacked, inclined buildings above an unbuilt Manhattan expressway. Though these and other proposals were never (meant to be) realized, two notable exceptions exist: the Nagakin Capsule Tower (1972) in Tokyo, designed by Kisho Kurokawa; and Habitat 67 in Montreal, designed by Moshe Safdie (1938–). The latter is much larger than the former, but it is also exceptional for the fact that it started as a student design, making it surely the largest thesis project ever built.

Safdie designed the project in his sixth and last year at McGill University, when he was originally set on a more typical thesis project—a parliament building in Jerusalem—but then switched gears to a "housing system" after frustration with both suburbs and urban high rises as inadequate solutions for housing families. The award-winning "A Three-Dimensional Modular Building System" developed into a preoccupation for Safdie even as he worked for other architects: Sandy van Ginkel in Montreal, and Louis I. Kahn in Philadelphia. In 1963, van Ginkel wooed Safdie back to Canada to work on the Expo 67 master plan, which he did for a little while before switching his focus back to Habitat.

The brute realities that all architects confront at each stage of a project turned Habitat into a smaller and different design than what Safdie produced at McGill and first proposed for Expo 67, but the modular basis stayed consistent throughout. What began as a proposal for 950 units in inclined A-frame structures was trimmed to 160 units, which pushed Safdie to redesign them into a cluster geometry of stacked modules. As built, 354 precast concrete modules made in a temporary factory next to the job site connect to create 158 residences in 15 different layouts, each one with a terrace on the roof of the unit below. The modules are articulated into three squat "pyramids" connected by pedestrian streets every four floors.

Habitat 67 was one of a trio of influential Expo 67 projects seen by fifty million visitors, the others being Frei Otto's German Pavilion and R. Buckminster Fuller's geodesic dome for the US Pavilion. Otto's tensile canopy was temporary, and the plastic covering on Fuller's dome went up in flames, but Habitat 67 remains a lasting influence, even though the acceptance of modular multifamily dwellings has progressed at what could be described generously as a snail's pace.

1968 FORD FOUNDATION

Kevin Roche John Dinkeloo and Associates ▸ New York City, United States

View south across the

atrium. Offices look onto

the atrium through glass

walls, while the executives,

perched at the top of the

12-story space, look back

toward the offices.

New York—particularly Manhattan and especially Midtown—is the ultimate American vertical city. Traditionally corporations and developers looked to maximize the available FAR (floor area ratio) on a lot, renting out what they didn't use and making a mark on the skyline through height and architecture. The Chrysler Building (1930) at Forty-Second Street and Lexington Avenue is an ideal example of a corporation's making a mark on the city, even if the carmaker hasn't occupied the building since the 1950s. Two blocks east of that iconic tower sits another auto-related building, one that eschews those traditional aspects of Midtown Manhattan architecture. Short rather than tall, devoted entirely to one tenant, and with half of its space given over to a garden, the Ford Foundation is as un-Manhattan as it is one of the most influential and memorable office buildings of the past century.

It makes sense that this very different headquarters is devoted to a philanthropic foundation rather than strictly a corporation. Started by Henry Ford and his son in 1936, the Ford Foundation was the largest institution of its kind when Kevin Roche (1922–) was hired in 1963 to design a new building. He purposely departed from the typical office floors they were leasing in a Madison Avenue high rise at the time with the aim of fostering a sense of community through design. The resulting building, carried out with his partner John Dinkeloo (1918–1981), has twelve stories of offices in shallow floor plates along the north and west sides of the square, mid-block plan, while the south and east exposures of the building have glass walls bringing sunlight to the full-height atrium capped by a large skylight. Materials inside and out are brown granite for walls and piers, and COR-TEN steel for the structure, as well as the framing of the glass walls.

Landscape architect Dan Kiley (1912–2004) designed the atrium as a subtropical conservatory that is a visual continuation of the Tudor City Parks on the east, and whose horizontal surfaces capably address the one-story grade change from the entrance on Forty-Third Street to Forty-Second Street. Unlike the privately owned public spaces (POPS) of the Seagram Building (see 1958) and other Midtown skyscrapers, the atrium is a fully private space that the Ford Foundation, at the urging of Roche, has opened to the public since its 1968 completion. It is one of the few places in Manhattan where (during the Ford Foundation's hours of operation, at least) the public can find respite from the noise, dirt, and heat or cold that are as distinctive a part of the city as is its skyline.

1969 FACULDADE DE ARQUITETURA E URBANISMO DA UNIVERSIDADE DE SÃO PAULO

João Batista Vilanova Artigas and Carlos Cascaldi ▸ São Paulo, Brazil

The school's multifunctional central hall. A grid of skylights covering the whole building brings natural light to the architecture studios on the top floor and the deep central hall.

Exterior view of cantilevered corner. The school of architecture proclaims itself and welcomes visitors by heroically lifting the top floors of concrete on sculpted columns.

In the late 1950s and early 1960s, Brazilian architect João Batista Vilanova Artigas (1915–1985) began what would become his third and most lasting phase. After an initial phase of primarily single-family houses with a strong Frank Lloyd Wright influence, followed by a second phase in which his work expanded into apartment buildings, his third phase focused on projects that were more public in nature. The most important building he realized during this period was the Faculdade de Arquitetura e Urbanismo da Universidade de São Paulo (FAU), carried out with frequent collaborator Carlos Cascaldi from 1961 until its inauguration in 1969.

Artigas's education in both engineering and architecture is evident in a number of buildings leading up to the FAU. Three recreational buildings in São Paulo—a football club, a tennis club, and a yacht club—share the following features: long, low rectangular buildings; ground floors that are predominantly open; upper floors encased behind exposed concrete walls lifted above the ground on columns. An important difference between the FAU and these predecessors arose from its educational program and Artigas's role in shaping the curriculum: he placed an open hall in the center of the building, what he envisioned as a space of democracy and dignity, where any activity could take place. To this day the space is used for exhibitions, lectures, performances, assemblies, and protests; the last is fitting given Artigas's own outspoken views on politics (in 1964 he was arrested under the Brazilian dictatorship for his Marxist views, relieved of teaching at the FAU, and exiled to Uruguay for two years).

Entry to the freestanding building is from just about any direction, in line with the architect's contention that the building should not have a front door. Beyond the sculpted concrete columns that hold up the raised concrete walls is a covered walkway that rings the whole building. Openings between glass-wall volumes lead directly to the central space that, like the whole building, is topped by skylights in a concrete grid. The spaces next to the central hall on the long sides—studios, classrooms, library, offices, etc.—are offset from each other by a half floor; a ramp at one of the short ends connects these floors and provides a vantage point for the grand scale of this democratic and pluralistic space.

Visitors to the building from 2008 until the 100th anniversary of Artigas's birth would have encountered skylights hung with blue tarp, an ad hoc means of catching pieces of the roof falling due to deferred maintenance. Thankfully the school started repairing the building piecemeal toward the architect's centennial celebrations that took place in 2015.

1970 CATEDRAL DE BRASÍLIA

Oscar Niemeyer ▸ **Brasília, Brazil**

Interior view toward altar. Although a circular plan prioritizes the center, the cathedral has a directionality that stems from the need to face east toward the altar.

Exterior view from the northeast. The cathedral is completely ringed by a reflecting pool that hints at the below-grade interior.

Everything about the planning of Brasília was rooted in abstraction: Brazil's new capital was positioned in the geographic center of the country, a departure from the preceding coastal capitals of Rio de Janeiro and Salvador; Lúcio Costa laid out the city like a cross, with one axis straight and the other curved so that it resembled a bird when seen from above; and the governmental buildings designed by Oscar Niemeyer (1907–2012) for President Juscelino Kubitschek (his client at Pampulha, 1947) took the form of large-scale gestures to be seen across the capital's monumental spaces. Brasília was inaugurated in April 1960, only four years after it was planned by Costa and designed by Niemeyer. Kubitschek likened the new capital to a cathedral and went so far as to call its builders *candangos* (the builders of the cathedral). It would be another ten years for the Catedral de Brasília, officially known as the Catedral Metropolitana de Nossa Senhora Aparecida, to be consecrated, partly because it was eventually funded by the faithful and not the state.

Originally planned to occupy its own monumental plaza where the capital's axes intersect, the cathedral was ultimately placed just south of the curved axis. The location prioritized the importance of the state over that of the church, but raised the issue of access to a circular church devoid of a front or back. Niemeyer solved the issue with a ramp perpendicular to the monumental curved axis; worshippers descend one level to a darkened corridor that leads to the 230-foot-diameter (70 m) space of light. Formed by sixteen parabolic concrete columns that converge in a ring and flare out above the roof, the cathedral has an obvious upward (heavenly) thrust. This sensation is even more pronounced inside, where the triangular openings between the columns—filled with glass in a hexagonal mesh—point to the ceiling and its ring of smaller triangular windows.

Integral with Niemeyer's sculptural church are three artworks: sculptures of the four evangelists by Dante Croce flank the entrance ramp; three bronze angels by Alfredo Ceschiatti with Dante Croce are suspended in the nave; and stained glass by Marianne Peretti illuminates the panels between the columns (she installed them in 1971, after the cathedral was consecrated, but modified her work in the late 1980s). Although these artworks add touches of color and symbolism to the church, Niemeyer envisioned the architecture itself as wholly expressing the House of God. He did so with the simplest of gestures: sixteen columns, a roof, and a floor embedded within the earth.

1971 PHILLIPS EXETER ACADEMY LIBRARY

Louis I. Kahn ▸ Exeter, New Hampshire, United States

Looking across the central three-story space. Note the drama and power of Kahn's masterful use of basic geometric forms.

The Phillips Exeter Academy Library is a brick box that sits prominently in the middle of the private school's New England campus, surrounded by early-twentieth-century Georgian buildings designed primarily by Ralph Adams Cram, including the Davis Library. Initially, the school had considered an addition to the library, but instead, hired Louis I. Kahn (1901–1974) in 1965 to design a new building. Kahn treated the exterior, with its simple grid of windows and solid, 45-degree corners, as an outcome of the building's interior function. Nevertheless, the exterior does little to ready visitors for the jaw-dropping interior.

Forty rectangular openings cover each of the library's exterior elevations—eight openings per floor; on the ground they connect to a wraparound arcade, at the top, a roof garden. On the other three floors the openings are split into two halves: glass on top, wood on bottom. The wood aligns with the 210 study carrels that are placed at the perimeter of each floor. Students can sit at the carrels and glance up at the sky through the top windows, open small shutters down below for campus views, or close the shutters for concentration. While the carrels may seem incidental to the design of the space, they are in fact integral to Kahn's conception of the whole: he envisioned librarians displaying books open to a particular page, so students would be intrigued enough to pick them up and carry them to a carrel to read. As part of this naïve but poetic scenario, Kahn placed the tables for displaying books at the interior edge of the three-story high central space, what can be seen as the inverse of the perimeter space of the carrels.

To get to the central space, visitors need to circumnavigate the arcade on the ground floor to find the hidden entrance, and then ascend curved steps to the first floor. The central space is a cubic void whose corner supports are set at 45 degrees to the space. These concrete columns resolve themselves at the top floor, where two deep concrete beams form an "X" across the void. Clerestory windows atop the building bring light to the central space, combined with light that spills through the grid of windows and enters via the grand gesture of the circular openings on the edges of the void. These circles-within-squares—a variation on the Vitruvian square-within-a-circle—put the stacks on display, an effect amplified by the solid wood railings, the insertions of mezzanine stacks between floors, and the relegation of carrels (and people) to the perimeter. Libraries have been about books traditionally, and this one expresses that in a way no other library has before or since.

1972 KIMBELL ART MUSEUM

Louis I. Kahn ▸ Fort Worth, Texas, United States

The north galleries with view into courtyard at left. The aluminum reflectors, which Kahn developed with lighting designer Richard Kelly, are one of the most distinctive and distinguished fixtures in any modern building.

View from the southwest. Kahn affectionately described the open vaults as unnecessary, but their inclusion creates an effective transition from the park to the museum interior.

The book that the Kimbell Art Museum published in 1975 on its three-year-old building was called *Light Is the Theme*, a fitting title for a building whose lighting effects are legendary, and whose architect was preoccupied with light for most of his career. "Silence and Light" was the title of a lecture given by Louis I. Kahn (1901–1974) in the late 1960s. These two elements—the former immeasurable and the latter the "giver of presence," in Kahn's words—come together poetically in this much-admired museum in Fort Worth's Cultural District.

From the moment Kahn was hired by museum director Richard F. Brown, the architect had in mind repetitive, vaulted spaces rather than open-plan layouts as in his Yale University Art Gallery (1953). The concrete vaults, in concert with concrete columns, travertine walls, and wood floors, define rooms with a scale and texture appropriate to Kay and Velma Kimbell's collection of paintings. What makes the intimate, room-sized galleries so beloved are the vaults' form—a shallow cycloid, not a half-circle—and the natural light that enters the spaces through a slit at their apex. Both of these traits were possible because the vaults were treated by Kahn and his structural engineer August Komendant as post-tensioned, reinforced concrete shells with intermediate struts, not load-bearing vaults. Knowing that direct sunlight harms paintings, Kahn added a custom, wing-shaped aluminum reflector to redirect sunlight across the underside of the vaults and provide a soft light to the paintings on display. Aluminum trays in the low ceiling between the vaults house the mechanical ducts and electrical conduits—the famous "servant" spaces Kahn was known for.

Kahn designed numerous plans for the museum, each one made up of the vaulted "rooms" in different numbers, lengths, and configurations. The final plan consists of sixteen vaulted modules 23 feet (7 m) wide and 100 feet (30 m) long, with three of them cut in the middle for small courtyards. The modules are grouped into three sections, with the westernmost vaults left open to the elements; these porches face Amon Carter Park and its newest addition, the Piano Pavilion (2013) designed by Renzo Piano.

Piano's low-slung, freestanding addition is the outcome of a two-plus-decade attempt to expand the museum, most controversially in 1989, with new wings designed by architect Romaldo Giurgola on the north and south sides of Kahn's building, an approach that was shot down by architects, critics, and, ultimately the museum's board. The uproar and eventual realization of a building that defers to its predecessor clearly illustrates the lasting appreciation of Kahn's building as an architectural masterpiece and one of the greatest settings for looking at art.

1973 SYDNEY OPERA HOUSE

Jørn Utzon ▸ **Sydney, Australia**

Detail of exterior shells. The roof's 2,194 precast concrete sections are covered in more than one million 5 inch (12 mm) white tiles.

The Opera House seen from the north. Utzon envisioned the building as a light sculptural roof perched above the heavy mass of the artificial plateau below.

Without a doubt, the Sydney Opera House is the most recognizable building in *100 Years, 100 Buildings.* Even from space the sail-like white shells are immediately recognizable. Given the way the building seems to belong in its location, one would assume that Danish architect Jørn Utzon (1918–2008) had a solid grasp on the city and its natural context when he entered the opera house's open international competition in 1957, but amazingly he didn't set foot on Australian soil until six months *after* he was named the winner. In 1966, nine years after winning the competition but six years before the building's official opening on October 20, 1973, Utzon left Australia never to return, having withdrawn from a project whose frustrations and heartache were in proportion to its benefits and praise.

Upon winning the competition, Utzon was faced with turning his freehand sketches into built reality. Most important, the three halls that rose from the podium had to be acoustically engineered for performances, and the cluster of curved white roofs had to find some basis in geometry so their forces could be measured, analyzed, and engineered for construction out of concrete. The latter has justly received the most attention, partly because they are the main image of the building, but also because the opera venues, like most of the interiors, fell to another architect after Utzon withdrew. Two months after winning the competition, Utzon paired up with structural engineer Ove Arup; five years later they had worked out a disciplined solution based on overlapping spheres of different sizes. Utzon opened an office in Australia the following year with Ove Arup following suit, even though the engineers were running the job at a loss and tensions between the two firms were flaring over authorship. Those tensions were nothing compared to the ones between Utzon and David Hughes, the NSW Minister for Public Works, who the architect single-handedly blamed for his departure.

Utzon would never return to Sydney to see in person the building that made him famous, and though the interiors fall short of the continuity and creativity of his original designs, and its final cost (fourteen times the initial budget) make expensive icons since pale in comparison, Sydney, Australia, and much of the exciting architecture produced there since would be unimaginable without Utzon's Sydney Opera House.

1974 HEDMARKSMUSEET

Sverre Fehn ▸ Hamar, Norway

Museum interior. Two-thirds of the former barn is a "cold" museum, open to the elements, with new walkways and rooms inserted above the ruins.

Courtyard view. A curving ramp takes visitors above some of the site's archaeological remains before delivering them into the building's south wing.

In the middle of the twentieth century, it could be said that architecture had an antagonistic relationship toward history, with contemporary buildings often at odds with their historical contexts. Yet there was a brief time in the late 1960s and early 1970s when some architects expressed a more sensitive relationship with history, clearly defining what was new and what was old in their projects. A good example is the work that Norwegian architect Sverre Fehn (1924–2009) carried out in Hamar from 1967 until 2005.

Before it was the Hedmarksmuseet, the late twelfth-century buildings near Mjøsa lake served as a bishop's manor. Faced with the choice of immediate repairs or demolition, a former student of Fehn's approached the architect in 1967 with the idea of transforming the U-shaped barn into a museum. Fehn visited the site with a structural engineer and together they figured out a way to stabilize the walls, beginning a long process of transforming the building into a constructed landscape where old and new coexist through mutual respect and the layering of one upon the other.

From the outside the changes are hard to decipher, since new glass fills the existing openings and new roofs follow the form and materials of the old ones. Yet that subtlety is abandoned in the courtyard, where a curving, boomerang-shaped concrete ramp gently rises from the ground, above the archaeological finds of the courtyard, and into the foyer of the lecture hall within the south wing. With offices and space for temporary exhibitions, the south wing is the only one heated; the west and north wings are open to make a "cold" museum traversed by concrete walkways that float between the floors of the original barn and the wood trusses of the modern roof. For Fehn, the bridges and ramps were horizons inserted between heaven and earth, where the latter's decay is slowed by these interventions.

The Hedmarksmuseet opened in 1974, but as mentioned, Fehn worked on it until he was over eighty years old. Most significantly, he added two outbuildings east of the barn, one whose serrated wood and glass walls and roof are clearly contemporary yet still fit with his idea of respectfully layering the new over the old. A different tactic can be seen in Lund+Slaatto Architects' cover over the cathedral ruin at the Hedmarksmuseet, completed in 1998: the technological construction of glass and steel approximates the form of the cathedral before its ruined state, a ghostly illustration of the past that overpowers what little remains. There is no right and wrong way to cap a ruin, but Hedmarksmuseet is one of the few places where different strategies can be compared side by side.

1975 MULTIHALLE

Frei Otto ▸ Mannheim, Germany

German architect and engineer Frei Otto (1925–2015) was one of the most creative and influential designers of the past hundred years, a strong proponent of the design philosophy less is more. Focused squarely on various forms of lightweight construction, Otto collaborated with other architects to create enclosures that appeared light enough to be buoyant. He found inspiration in nature, particularly soap bubbles, and geared his research toward applying the principles found in natural systems to architectural forms. First gaining international renown for two cable-net structures—the German Pavilion at the Expo 67 in Montreal (with Rolf Gutbrod) and the roofing of the main sports facilities for the 1972 Olympic Games in Munich (with Günter Behnisch)—one of Otto's most exceptional projects is the gridshell construction of the Multihalle created for the 1975 German Federal Garden Exhibition in Mannheim.

Whereas the complex cable-net projects preceding the Multihalle have an overt structural logic—glass and fabric surfaces suspended from large steel masts via cables—the gridshell technique merges form, structure, and surface into one seamless construction. Although not invented by Otto, the technique was first applied by Otto in a small dome for the German Building Exhibition in Essen in 1962, and then as a cover for a lecture hall within his 1967 German Pavilion in Montreal.

In gridshell construction, thin pieces of wood are laid flat in a grid and then gradually lifted into place to form a double-curved shell. Like Antoni Gaudí decades before him (see 1917), Otto found the optimal form for the gridshells by building models with suspended chains, such that the tension forces of the chains mimicked the compression forces of the final structure. Engineers at Ove Arup & Partners tested the resulting structural design with rudimentary computer software, making it a pioneering work in the use of computers for structural engineering, a necessity for many of the buildings that make up the balance of *100 Years, 100 Buildings*.

As in his other projects, Otto's work on the Multihalle was a collaboration: in this instance with architects Carlfried Mutschler and Partners, which won a 1970 competition for the exhibition master plan of Mannheim's Herzogenriedpark. They envisioned the Multihalle as a multipurpose hall and restaurant that could be used for various functions once the exhibition closed, meaning it would be a permanent addition to the city, not a temporary structure like Otto's Expo 67 tent. Nestled among trees in the northwest corner of the 80 acre (32 hectare) park, the amoebalike Multihalle was given landmark protection in 1998, and now a portion of its 80,000 square feet (7,400 sq. m) is occupied partially by a restaurant.

1976 BAGSVÆRD CHURCH

Jørn Utzon ▸ **Bagsværd, Denmark**

Looking south across the nave. In addition to the architecture, Utzon designed the furnishings, selecting a light wood that complements the white surfaces of the ceilings, walls, and floor.

One of the most important things I learned in architecture school was how to think and learn "in section," meaning the vertical dimension and shape of a space. Plans (the horizontal dimension) were important, but when it came to designing spaces—rooms, corridors, courtyards, etc.—sections took priority. By their nature, plans correspond to the movement of people through spaces, while sections relate to how people experience those spaces. One architect who surely designed in section more than plan was Denmark's Jørn Utzon (1918–2008), and the Evangelical-Lutheran church he designed for Bagsværd, a suburb of Copenhagen, is the best illustration of this approach.

The plan of Bagsværd Church is a long rectangle that corresponds to its site. Each long side is given over to a narrow corridor that runs the length of the building, with the southern end, which faces the parking lot across the street, broken in places for access from the exterior. Perpendicular pathways connect these long corridors and break the plan into smaller spaces: the western end is given over to the congregation space and a chapel, while the east is devoted to the parish hall, a meeting room, offices, and a garden. The basic plan is reflected in an equally simple exterior, which is made up of a grid of columns filled in with whitish precast concrete panels that gives the religious building a quasi-industrial appearance. Variation in the primarily solid exterior happens in the gable-shaped skylights above the corridors, a large clerestory window facing west, and the stepping of the columns and panels at the nave. Further, the top portions of the precast panels are covered in glazed tiles; their varying heights are subtle hints at the nonrectilinear section of the interior space.

Expectations downplayed by the impenetrable exterior, the interior of the church is a marvel, set off by the undulating surfaces of the white ceilings and light that infiltrates from an invisible source (actually the western clerestory glimpsed outside). Utzon likened the curved ceilings to clouds, but they are materially the antithesis: curved sections of poured-in-place concrete (still exhibiting the rough wooden formwork underneath the paint) span from one sidewall to the other, a full 55 feet (17 m). Not as structurally daring or complicated as the Sydney Opera House (see 1973), these surfaces are nevertheless an amazing feat at only 5 inches (12 cm) thick. Since the ends of each "cloud" are out of sight, visitors cannot fully grasp the technical accomplishment. But in section, the shape of the space is more wavelike than cloudlike, formed as it is by the light flowing across the ceiling's crests and troughs.

1977 CENTRE GEORGES POMPIDOU

Renzo Piano and Richard Rogers ▸ Paris, France

West elevation facing Rue du Renard. The cantilevered "gerberettes" hold the building's service guts, executed like a paint-by-numbers: blue for air, green for water, red for elevators, and yellow for electricity.

Elevation facing the plaza on the east. The suspended escalators snake up the gridded structure, the architectural image most associated with the Centre Georges Pompidou.

It is telling that in 1971, when an open, international competition was held for a new interdisciplinary cultural institution on Plateau Beaubourg in Paris, the eventual winning team was formed by engineer Edmund "Ted" Happold, then a partner at Ove Arup & Partners in London. An embrace of modern technology and a daring expression of the structural and mechanical engineering that all buildings rely on, the Centre Georges Pompidou launched the separate but prolific careers of architects Renzo Piano (1937–) and Richard Rogers (1933–).

The mandate for a building combining a museum, library, and other cultural facilities came from Georges Pompidou six months into his French presidency, buoyed by the optimism following the civil unrest of May 1968. When it came time for the jury, which included architects Philip Johnson and Jean Prouvé, to make a selection, the slightly sunken plaza set aside for half of the large site in the Piano and Rogers scheme was one consideration that put them above the 680 other submissions. Other positive aspects of the design were the flexibility afforded by the long-span steel structure and the lively and animated exterior that resulted from essentially turning the building inside out.

The building houses seven above-grade floors with open floor plates of 165 feet (50 m) by 560 feet (170 m)—roughly the same size as the plaza, which can be considered an eighth floor, and is one of the liveliest public spaces in Paris. The open floors are enabled by 150-foot-long (45 m) steel beams engineered by Happold and fellow Arup colleague Peter Rice (who had just come off of working on the Sydney Opera House); the latter was instrumental in the building's most memorable structural piece: the cast steel "gerberettes" that cantilever from the columns on the long east and west sides of the building.

Since the building was inaugurated on January 31, 1977, Renzo Piano has returned to execute three projects related to the Pompidou: the Institut de Recherche et Coordination Acoustique/Musique (IRCAM, 1990) faces the plaza on the south; Atelier Brancusi (1996), the reconstruction of Constantin Brancusi's studio, is situated at the plaza's north end; and from 1997 to 2000 the Renzo Piano Building Workshop restored and renovated the whole Centre Georges Pompidou, work that moved offices off-site, expanded the museum, and reworked the library. Unfortunately, one result of the reshuffling is that the building's signature escalators are only available to those who gain entry to the museum; it is no longer a free ride to the top floor and its grand views over the rooftops of Paris.

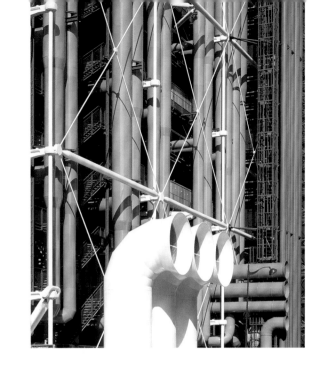

1978 BRION-VEGA CEMETERY

Carlo Scarpa ▸ San Vito d'Altivole, Italy

Looking north from meditation pavilion. The three structures in the family cemetery sit at the three points of an "L" with the angled concrete bridge of the *arcosolium* acting as a hinge between the other two.

Chapel seen from the west. The only building proper in the cemetery is a square chapel set into a pool near the entrance from the road.

Carlo Scarpa (1906–1978) once remarked in his plainspoken manner, "I never finish my work." In the case of the cemetery he designed for Giuseppe Brion, cofounder of the Brionvega electronics company, the words were prophetic. Though the project was substantially complete in 1972, Scarpa tinkered with it until he died in 1978 due to complications from a fall into an excavated pit at the construction site. He now resides permanently in an inside corner of the cemetery, beneath a marker that is modest (a flat stone slab with grooves that channel rainwater to a small opening) yet exudes the considerations Scarpa pursued in his buildings and interiors.

Though often called an architect, Scarpa was never certified as one; he studied fine arts and refused to sit for the architectural exams after World War II. Practically, this meant he had to work with architects on building commissions; it also meant much of his focus was devoted to interior renovations, where he confronted history on a regular basis, most notably in the Castelvecchio (1964) in Verona. Combined with his upbringing in Venice and elsewhere in the Veneto, his projects tended to grapple with tradition, even if not in the most immediate ways. Clearly modern, his intensely detailed and personal style of architecture resounds with the sensations of archaic time, like Louis I. Kahn, who was a great admirer of Scarpa's work. The Brion-Vega Cemetery can be seen as the summation of the poetry he erected in concrete and other materials.

The cemetery occupies a roughly half-acre (one-fifth hectare), L-shaped plot of land next to the existing San Vito d'Altivole cemetery. Scarpa walled off the new cemetery from the surrounding landscape and provided two points of access: one directly from the road and one through the old cemetery; the latter is recommended, for it reinforces the differences between the traditional village cemetery and Scarpa's modern version. Through the porch is a wall with an opening formed by two interlocking circles, a recurring motif in Scarpa's buildings. From here a right turn leads to a pool and meditation pavilion, one of the three structures set intentionally yet leisurely about the landscape. A linear fountain points from the pool to the left, toward the second structure, a concrete bridge that Scarpa called the *arcosolium*, where Brion and his wife are buried. This highly articulated and vegetated structure is angled 45 degrees in plan toward the third structure, the chapel, a block of poured-in-place concrete; its intricate interior features an altar capped by a diamond-shaped ceiling and skylight with Scarpa's familiar stepping, much like his grave marker outside.

1979 THE ATHENEUM

Richard Meier ▸ New Harmony, Indiana, United States

Ramp up the second floor. Movement through the building via ramps and stairs provides ever-changing views of the town and the landscape, making the building as much an educational tool as what it contains.

The Atheneum seen from the south. Meier designed the building as a circuit that moves people through the galleries and then outside via a long stair (right) on the same axis with buildings of the old town.

New Harmony—population 945 in 1980, about one-fifth less thirty years later—is an unlikely place for a gleaming white, late-modern piece of architecture. Yet there in southern Indiana is where the Atheneum sits, raised above the floodplain of the nearby Wabash River on an earthen podium, like the Acropolis filtered through Le Corbusier. Opened to the public on October 10, 1979, as postmodernism was in the midst of overtaking architectural education and practice, it is unapologetically modern with a capital M: Richard Meier's (1934–) gridded, white, angular, glass-and-steel design is at odds with its surroundings yet completely in tune with them on deeper reading.

The project began in 1975, when Ralph G. Schwarz, president of Historic New Harmony, hired Meier, a New York architect, to create an entry point for explorations of the nineteenth-century town founded in 1814 by George Rapp's Harmony Society. The theosophical group moved back to Pennsylvania only one decade later, giving Welsh immigrant Robert Owen the canvas to build a settlement based on equality, progressive education, and communal living. The town that visitors see today is an assemblage of the two utopian visions layered with later residential and commercial buildings, and even a piece of modern architecture in Philip Johnson's Roofless Church (1960).

Located in the very northwest corner of the small town, the Atheneum (now run, as is the rest of the historic town, by the University of Southern Indiana) orients itself to three areas through openings, angles, ramps, and marks in the sloping landscape: the Wabash River to the west, the parking lot where visitors arrive on the south, and the old town on the east. Although the western path reaches to the river to recognize the importance of the waterway on life in the 1800s, most visitors today arrive by car, walking on axis toward a large, gridded white wall with the entry notched in the lower-left corner. Once inside the 15,000 square-foot (1,400 sq. m) building, visitors learn about the town through a short film in the Clowes Theatre and through artifacts spread across three small galleries, one of them behind an undulating wall that mimics the flow of the waters outside.

A shallow stair on the east—the strongest formal gesture on the outside of the building—is set at a slight angle to the street grid, directing people from the second floor to the restored frontier log cabins nearby. Although the Atheneum Visitors Center does not maintain this part of the architectural promenade (most visitors exit where they enter, renting golf carts by the parking lot to explore the town), the power of this gesture as a means of engaging the new building with its historical context is still tangible.

1980 THORNCROWN CHAPEL

E. Fay Jones ▸ Eureka Springs, Arkansas, United States

Beauty resides in repetition in this pilgrimage chapel nestled in the woods outside Eureka Springs, a resort village in the Ozarks of northwest Arkansas. Standard-size lumber—two-by-fours, two-by-sixes, and two-by-twelves—were assembled into diamond-shaped trusses and braces that repeat twenty-two times. The result is a small building that is wedded to its wooded context but stands out from it through a geometric rigor that is distinctly human and extremely poetic.

Nine years before the chapel opened on July 10, 1980, Jim Reed had purchased land along Highway 62 to build a home for his retirement. Yet when he and his wife noticed that the spot was popular with travelers admiring the Ozarks scenery, he opted to build a chapel that would, in his words, "give wayfarers a place to relax in an inspiring way." In homage to the wooded mountainside, architect E. Fay Jones (1921–2004) designed the chapel with standard pieces of southern pine lumber two men could easily carry through the woods. Trusses were assembled on the chapel's flagstone floor and lifted into place, enclosed by 425 windows on four sides and a line of skylights at the roof's apex. The crisscrossing of the wood members creates large diamond-shaped openings that take on a moiré effect as they recede in the distance. An unexpected detail occurs in the hollow steel joints that connect the two halves of the trusses and cross-braces down the middle of the space: their smaller diamond-shaped openings are a symbol of the infinite or perhaps the beyond, much like the cross of light at Tadao Ando's Church of the Light in Osaka (see 1989).

Thorncrown Chapel's importance and popularity is evident in the numerous awards it has garnered, particularly those from the American Institute of Architects, but also in the six million people who have made the pilgrimage to the buildings in the woods. Demand for weddings and worship services in the beautiful space led Reed to hire Jones again for a larger building more like a traditional church. As in other religious structures the architect designed after Thorncrown, the Worship Center, completed in 1989 just steps away from the chapel, reiterates the repetition of small structural members, yet this time the walls are solid save a large window behind the altar that frames the treetops of the surrounding mountains, the raison d'être for the buildings and their graceful designs.

View from the southwest. The hollow steel joints connecting the trusses create small diamond-shaped openings that run down the middle of the space.

1981 HAJJ TERMINAL

Skidmore, Owings & Merrill ▸ Jeddah, Saudi Arabia

The terminal structure seen from the tarmac. Steel cables suspended from 150-foot-tall (45 m) tapered concrete pylons support the tents, which are 110 feet (33 m) tall at their circular tips and 66 feet (20 m) at the bottom, where they meet the pylons.

Detail of the fiberglass tents. During the day the white tents give a soft glow to the spaces below, but in the evening uplighting on the tents gives their undersides a pleasant glow.

As one of the Five Pillars of Islam, Muslims must carry out the Hajj, the annual pilgrimage to Mecca, at least once in their lifetime. When Islamic governments offered to sponsor pilgrimage flights, a terminal catering to the hundreds of thousands of pilgrims heading to Mecca in the last month of the Islamic calendar was needed. In 1974, the Saudi government and Washington, DC–based Airways Engineering Corporation hired the New York City office of Skidmore, Owings & Merrill (SOM) to program King Abdulaziz International Airport, the centerpiece of which is the Hajj Terminal, designed by partners Gordon Wildermuth, Gordon Bunshaft, and Fazlur Khan.

Wildermuth started on the project and, with SOM colleagues, observed the Hajj firsthand, an experience that made it clear the terminal would have to meet an atypical set of design principles. Accommodation for up to 80,000 people was needed at any given time for the two months the terminal would be in service, since pilgrims would deplane but then need to wait up to thirty-six hours for a 45-mile (72 km) bus ride to Mecca. This and other considerations led to a terminal that would be primarily open, with air-conditioning only in limited areas. In an early scheme, the open terminal was covered by concrete shell "sun umbrellas" that recalled the work space Frank Lloyd Wright designed for Johnson Wax (see 1950), but in 1977 Bunshaft and Khan came on board and the design headed in a direction that was modern yet infused with the region's vernacular forms.

The Hajj Terminal is made up of 210 Teflon-coated fiberglass tents grouped into ten modules that cover 105 acres (42 hectares), split into two rectangular areas astride an access road. The size of the terminal footprint and height of the tents give the shaded space an impressive scale. A combination of natural ventilation and reflective white material keeps the temperature inside the tent around 80 degrees Fahrenheit (27 degrees Celsius), even when the outside temperature reaches 130 degrees Fahrenheit (54 degrees Celsius).

Hajj Terminal was dedicated on April 12, 1981, when 950,000 pilgrims were expected to pass through on their way to Mecca. Annual increases in their numbers taxed the terminal to the point that it was modernized in time for the 2010 Hajj, when a staggering 6.2 million pilgrims made the trip via the tented space. With both Hajj and Umrah pilgrims making the annual trip, the latter at any time of the year, King Abdulaziz added another terminal that will handle thirty million passengers annually. Unfortunately the new terminal does not learn from the lessons of the Hajj Terminal: that a modern facility can address the region's culture and climate in sensitive yet creative ways.

1982 SESC POMPÉIA

Lina Bo Bardi ▸ **São Paulo, Brazil**

Theater foyer. The renovated "general activities pavilion" subtly layers new upon old, including new levels inserted into the old shell and, here, a glass roof where the old one caved in.

The sports facilities seen from the west. A boardwalk built over the Águas Pretas creek leads past the renovated buildings on the left to the new concrete buildings connected by futuristic bridges.

Between 1946, when Lina Bo Bardi (1914–1992) emigrated from Italy to Brazil, and 1977, when she received the commission for the SESC (Serviço Social do Comércio), the population of São Paulo increased from 1.6 million to nearly 8 million. In 1946 the SESC was founded as a private, nonprofit entity whose budget comes from a payroll tax levied on Brazilian companies, in order to provide sports facilities, libraries, and various programs for the employees of those companies. As the population grew so did SESC's budget, resulting in Bo Bardi's construction on the site of a decommissioned manufacturing facility in inner São Paulo's Pompéia neighborhood.

Bo Bardi could have razed the existing brick warehouses to create a tabula rasa, but in keeping with the client's wishes, she integrated the various facilities—library, theater and exhibition spaces, restaurant, beer garden, and reflecting pool—into the existing structures. Her hand within these spaces is light, primarily made up of concrete floors, walls, and stairs inserted into the exposed shells; she also designed the furnishings throughout. Where a roof caved in years before, she covered the opening with glass, a tactic that recalls Sverre Fehn's work at the Hedmarksmuseet (see 1974).

Although the SESC opened its renovated "general activities pavilion" to the public in 1982, a lull in construction delayed the completion of the sports facilities for another four years. Faced with limited space, Bo Bardi had no choice but to build up. Just as she let the existing buildings determine some of her design for the cultural facilities, she took the site constraints as a given and split the new building into two concrete high rises. The larger volume houses a pool on the ground floor and four sports courts above it, each floor with a ceiling height of approximately 40 feet (12 m), with irregular openings in the walls meant to evoke prehistoric caves when seen from inside. The 11-story tower with the locker rooms and other subsidiary spaces has a smaller footprint, floors with lower ceilings, an irregular grid of square windows, and is turned 45 degrees to its heavier counterpart. To reach the pool and ball courts people ascend elevators and stairs in the smaller building and traverse the V- and Y-shaped walkways—concrete elements that give the project a futuristic image. Regardless of these striking connectors, a third tower, the circular water tower, has become the project's icon, memorably depicted in a drawing by Bo Bardi where flowers spill out of the top, perfectly illustrating the SESC Pompéia's standing within its community.

1983 NATIONAL ASSEMBLY BUILDING

Louis I. Kahn ▸ Dhaka, Bangladesh

View of the National Assembly Building from the hostel buildings. The buildings of brick and concrete are united by geometric openings and an artificial lake that channels rainwater away from the site into a nearby river.

Corridor in the National Assembly Building. Kahn gave the circulation spaces an impressive scale, acknowledging that politics happen in these informal spaces, not just in the chamber.

The year 1962 was busy for Louis I. Kahn (1901–1974). In addition to receiving commissions for two large projects on the Indian subcontinent—the Indian Institute of Management (1974) in Ahmedabad and the master plan for Sher-E-Bangla-Nagar, the second capital of Pakistan, later Bangladesh—his son Nathaniel Kahn was born. In 2003 Kahn released *My Architect: A Son's Journey*, a documentary that explores his father's life through interviews with friends, family, and colleagues, but also through visits to many of his buildings. Nathaniel's greatest understanding of his father comes at the end of the film, during a visit to Bangladesh and Sher-E-Bangla-Nagar, better known as the National Assembly complex (completed in 1983, nine years after Kahn was found dead in New York's Penn Station); there he at last grasps his father's generous nature and his ability to give form to something intangible, in this case independence, as achieved by Bangladesh in 1971.

Bangladesh's National Assembly complex as built in the years before and after the civil war of 1971 is composed of two major parts: the sizable National Assembly Building made of concrete and marble, and the flanking hostels, dining halls, and other related buildings made of brick. Both components are located on an artificial lake, with the assembly given prominence through its scale and central location. The landscape ties the two parts into one complex, as do the forms of the buildings, composed of basic geometric shapes (circle, square, and triangle). These shapes are evident throughout the overall plan, and are also found in the openings of both interior and exterior walls. The most remarkable geometric composition is the assembly with an octagonal space at its center (the chamber), and square and cylindrical rooms of different sizes and functions (offices, lounge, dining hall, prayer room) at the perimeter; in between is a circulation zone, the complex interplay of the central and peripheral spaces. Light enters the chamber through large circular openings above the parasol ceiling, while "hollow columns," as Kahn called them, do the same for the circulation and perimeter spaces.

Kahn apparently found much inspiration in the local architecture. His design was also influenced by the hot and humid climate. Yet the modern massing and large geometric openings resonate as abstract patterns in the architect's personal manner, and, like Le Corbusier in Ahmedabad (1954), spaces open to the elements allow natural breezes as well as, unfortunately, monsoons. Despite these critiques, the monumentality and memorability of the complex, particularly the National Assembly Building, is a dramatic and lasting gift from a great architect to a young nation.

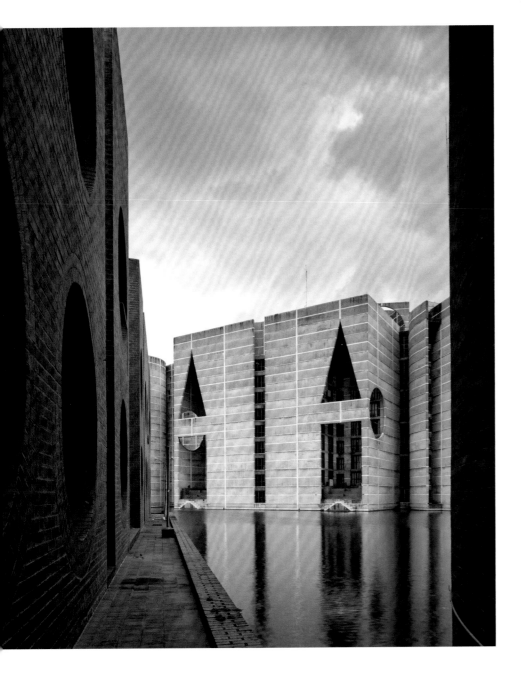

1984 NEUE STAATSGALERIE

James Stirling Michael Wilford and Associates ▸ Stuttgart, Germany

The entry plaza. The green mullions and curved glass signal the entrance, while the red railings beyond lead to the central courtyard.

Central courtyard. The space below is accessible from inside the museum, but the ramp is a public thoroughfare that connects the urban areas east and west, high and low.

Most of the attention given to the 1977 competition-winning design by James Stirling (1926–1992) and Michael Wilford (1938–) for an addition to the 1843 Staatsgalerie (State Gallery) has focused on its postmodern qualities, particularly in its playful use of architectural elements: colorful balustrades and exposed structure, oversize columns, and stone blocks that appear to tumble from the facade. But the power of their design is in its plan, which sensitively inserts the 165,000 square-foot (15,300 sq. m) building into Stuttgart's "Cultural Mile," resulting in one of the most successful symbioses of architecture and urban design in the last half of the twentieth century.

Architecturally, the plan harks back to, among other precedents, Karl Friedrich Schinkel's famous Altes Museum (1830) in Berlin, which has an enclosed circular space at the center of its rectangular plan; at the Neue Staatsgalerie, the central space is an open-air rotunda that acts as a void. While it can be accessed from the museum, this central space serves mainly as a curling conduit for moving pedestrians from the city center on the west to the elevated residential areas on the east—and vice versa. Here is where the urban design merits of the building are apparent, since the building knits together its context in a way that echoes other parts of the highly walkable city. Two later additions—a history museum and a school for music and art, also designed by Stirling and Wilford—complete the Cultural Mile, extend the architectural language of the 1984 building and, more important, continue the approach of using outdoor spaces to connect different areas of the city.

For those visiting the Neue Staatsgalerie, entry happens from the raised plaza that faces the eight lanes of traffic to the west, past a glass wall that curves like a grand piano and is framed with bright-green mullions. The colorful palette and playful touches continue inside with green rubber flooring and concrete columns with mushroom capitals. The galleries, on the other hand, are more sedate affairs, connected by enfilades, like the original Staatsgalerie, instead of corridors, and are capped by glass ceilings that bring in plenty of daylight and focus attention on the art, green mullions notwithstanding.

1985 HONGKONG AND SHANGHAI BANK CORPORATION HEADQUARTERS

Norman Foster ▸ **Hong Kong, China**

View from the northeast. Norman Foster's competition-winning design gave HSBC a striking new identity a dozen years before Hong Kong was returned to China.

An architectural competition enables a client to understand how architects think by seeing how their needs are addressed, resulting in a building that can differ from the competition design in its smallest details to the overall form. In the case of the 1979 invited competition for the Hongkong and Shanghai Bank Corporation (HSBC) Headquarters, Norman Foster's (1935–) winning design is conceptually similar yet decidedly different from the building that opened for business in 1985.

Given that its previous headquarters, while not an architectural masterpiece, was featured on its logo, in postcards, and even on the $100 bank note, something distinctive would have to replace it. Furthermore, the roughly five years of construction would have to allow corporate and banking operations to continue uninterrupted. Foster designed a system in which half of the tower's concrete cores, connected by two-story-high trusses and suspended floor plates *above* the existing banking hall, would rise on the east and west sides of the site. Once the new tower reached its apex, the banking hall and the north tower would be demolished so that the new building could be completed outward and downward. In hindsight this strategy was wishful thinking, but Foster's innovative thinking impressed HSBC enough that the completed building retained the architectural expression born from this approach.

Although the bankers—and the famous bronze lions—moved to a nearby building and the bank's 1966 annex was converted to a banking hall for the duration of the construction, Foster's design retained the original outer cores and intermittent trusses. As executed, the details in these two areas differ dramatically: the columns changed from concrete to steel and moved inward, and the trusses cantilevered from the columns to contain the cores on the outside and meet in the building's middle. Foster's approach made a major impact on the interior through the creation of five vertical zones, each with a double-height lobby and escalators connecting the floors.

Some of the longest escalators in existence at the time connect the open plaza beneath the building to HSBC's public lobby three stories overhead, piercing the plaza's glass ceiling, which receives natural light through a system of mirrors mounted at the top of the ten-story atrium, one of many design elements that address the building's feng shui. At various points along the design and construction process, feng shui masters were consulted on everything from the color of the building and the location of the escalators to the final placement of the old building's lions. Combined with the bamboo scaffolding that wrapped the high-tech building during its construction, the feng shui considerations point to the coexistence of the traditional and the modern in a building that looks purely high-tech.

1986 MUSEO NACIONAL DE ARTE ROMANO

Rafael Moneo ▸ **Mérida, Spain**

Looking west down the "nave." The brick arches generally recall Roman construction, but specifically they resemble those of the archaeological remains across from the museum.

The many conquests of ancient Rome left their mark on lands well beyond Italy, so that Britain, France, Spain, and other countries must often deal with the complexities of building on top of Roman ruins. A common tactic when preserving archaeological ruins, Roman or otherwise, is to cover them with a long-span structure and a translucent material that provides protection from the elements, while allowing some natural light to illuminate the ruins. It's an approach that creates a strong contrast between old and new, something that Rafael Moneo (1937–) shied away from in his design for the Museo Nacional de Arte Romano, sited amid the ruins of an ancient Roman colony.

Emerita Augusta, founded in 25 BC by Emperor Augustus upon his conquest of Hispania, eventually became the capital of the Roman province of Lusitania. Now present-day Mérida, its extraordinary collection of well-preserved archaeological remains, including a theater, amphitheater, forum, temples, houses, and numerous other structures, were added to the UNESCO World Heritage List in 1993. Nearly two decades earlier, in 1975, the Museo Nacional de Arte Romano was created to celebrate the city's bimillenary. Five years later, Moneo was hired to design a museum to house the artifacts that had been discovered during archaeological excavations; it was inaugurated September 19, 1986.

Moneo approached the museum design with a plan and structure similar to—but not a duplicate of—the load-bearing masonry system of the ruins below: the building is all brick, its main galleries articulated as parallel walls expressed as buttressed piers on the exterior. Differences between old and new are found in the details and the orientation, with very little mortar visible in the new walls that sit perpendicular to the street grid and therefore at an angle to the ruins. The ruins are visible in the cellar level and in the opening between the two volumes of the museum, where a sunken Roman street is visible from the street above. Entrance to the museum is through the smaller volume that faces the theater and amphitheater, and from here a walkway traverses the Roman road into the main, three-story volume of the museum. An off-center, navelike space cuts through the parallel brick walls to form niches on the shallow side for statues and other large artifacts, and on the deep side, three floors of galleries for smaller objects, such as ceramics, glass, and mosaics. A combination of skylights and clerestory windows brings plenty of light to the "nave," while a series of skylights on one wall bring daylight to the Roman ruins in the cellar, where new and old merge through the medium of masonry.

1987 INSTITUT DU MONDE ARABE

Jean Nouvel ▸ Paris, France

The south elevation. When the sun hits the building, as in this photo, the diaphragms of the 240 square *mashrabiyas* narrow to restrict the direct sunlight entering the building.

The first of French President François Mitterrand's seven *Grands Projets* to be completed, the Institut du Monde Arabe (Arab World Institute) is a remarkable high-tech expression of the Arab world, free of the pastiche of Islamic elements (arches, niches, domes) that could have easily occurred during the heyday of postmodernism. Some credit can go to the Parisian government, whose aim was twofold: improve the poor image of Arab culture in France and reinforce France's understanding of that part of the world. The winning design by Jean Nouvel (1945–), with Gilbert Lezenes, Pierre Soria, and Architecture Studio, achieves these aims through careful responses to the site and novel techniques for expressing Arab culture.

The institute is located on the Left Bank between the Seine and the Jussieu Campus of the University Pierre et Marie Curie. The campus to the south is very un-Parisian, with large blocks and modern buildings, while the Île Saint-Louis and Île de la Cité, home to Notre Dame de Paris, sit in the river to the north. Nouvel responded to this varied context by splitting the building into two volumes: a nine-story rectangular bar on the south and a shorter tapered volume on the north that follows the curve of the Seine. A glass-and-aluminum curtain wall with tight, horizontal mullions faces the Seine, while prized views of the historical islands in the Seine can be had from the rooftop terrace.

If the northern volume is about the flow of the Seine and views of the historical city, the southern bar is where the Arab expression concentrates. A flat glass facade composed of a grid of 240 square *mashrabiyas* filters the sunlight entering the building, an effect modulated by photosensitive diaphragms. The intricate pattern of diamonds, hexagons, and circles, recalling Islamic motifs without mimicking them, is mirrored in the paving of the plaza that sits between the museum and the north edge of the Jussieu Campus. The paving also echoes the below-grade portions of the project, particularly the hypostyle hall with its tightly spaced round columns.

The plaza to the south gives entry to the building; in between the two volumes is a narrow, full-height slot with a walkway that leads to another entrance. Inside are a museum, exhibition halls, library, documentation center, auditorium, restaurant, cafeteria, and High Council Hall, while overlapping both halves of the building is a square courtyard open to the sky. Just as the exterior is all aluminum and glass, the interiors designed by Nouvel are gray and transparent, with more glass and aluminum prevailing. Although the building is an overarching high-tech environment, the operable *mashrabiyas* turn the expression of Arab culture into streaks of light that imbue the spaces with a rich texture that belies its flatness.

1988 MUSEU BRASILEIRO DA ESCULTURA

Paulo Mendes da Rocha ▸ São Paulo, Brazil

General view from the southeast. A triangular pool and row of trees are some of the few soft touches of the hardscape plaza above the museum.

View under the concrete bar. The tiered surfaces of the plaza relate to the museum functions below and provide areas of activity.

Thirty years before he completed the Museu Brasileiro da Escultura (MuBE, the Brazilian Museum of Sculpture) in São Paulo, Brazilian architect Paulo Mendes da Rocha (1928–) had realized two buildings designed as large slabs of concrete over highly articulated ground planes: the flying saucer–like gymnasium of the Paulistano Athletic Club (1958), also in São Paulo, and the Brazilian Pavilion at Expo 70 in Osaka, Japan. He would continue defining outdoor space via an overhead mass in subsequent projects (Patriarca Square, 1992, is a highlight), but his most successful execution occurred at MuBE through its scale, simplicity, and setting.

The museum is located on a large trapezoidal lot in the city's wealthy Jardim Europa neighborhood. The block on Avenida Europa was already home to the Museum of Image and Sound when the 1.7-acre (0.7-hectare) lot became available in the mid-1980s for development. The neighborhood association lobbied for another museum and the city gave in and donated the land. But when Mendes da Rocha was hired the museum did not have a collection, so he proposed turning the site into a public garden and placing the museum below it. As realized, the MuBE is just that, a primarily hardscape garden that steps down from one corner of the site to the other, with its subtle touches of green and blue—trees, grass, and a triangular reflecting pool, all designed by Roberto Burle Marx—pushed to the edges. If not for the rectangular concrete slab 200 feet long by 40 feet wide (61 × 12 m) hovering just 7½ feet (2.3 m) above the ground at its high point, the museum would disappear. The program-free concrete slab gives the building presence while also providing shade and shelter on the otherwise open public plaza.

Entry to the below-grade museum is from the lowest level of the plaza, accessible from the street perpendicular to Avenida Europa, a ramp by the triangular pool, a ramp alongside the far leg of the 200 foot long slab, and from a stepped amphitheater underneath the slab. The last is a particularly important element, as it gives the garden some semblance of function and a release from the compression the concrete slab impacts on the space beneath it. The shaping of the hardscape also relates to the museum functions below; for example, the tall gallery spaces correspond to the high points of the plaza, and the sunken theater caps the shorter service zone. Unbeknownst to those just visiting the garden, the partially covered surface is the interface between the museum and the city.

1989 CHURCH OF THE LIGHT

Tadao Ando ▸ Ibaraki-shi, Osaka, Japan

Church interior. The rows of pews slope down to the altar and the glowing cross that gives the impression of something beyond, something intangible and out of reach.

Sunday school interior. Although the light is less dramatic, the Sunday school has a similarly proportioned space punctured by an angled wall just like the church.

As famous for being a former professional boxer and a self-taught architect (he traveled the world to visit buildings for his education rather than attending architecture school), as for his meticulous concrete walls, Tadao Ando (1941–) received international acclaim in the late 1980s and early 1990s when he realized three small religious buildings in Japan. In fact, deciding between the Church of the Light (Ibaraki Kasugaoka Church) in suburban Osaka, the Water Temple (1991) on Awaji Island, and the Church on the Water (1988) in Hokkaido for this book was no easy task. Each project transforms Ando's preferred material of concrete into poetic, existential experiences through the manipulation of light, views, and, in two cases, water. The Church of the Light, in addition to being the most convenient to visit (the only one of the three I have visited), is most exceptional for imbuing a simple form with cosmic meaning.

Ando was hired in 1987 by the Reverend Noboru Karukome to design a church for the small Ibaraki Kasugaoka congregation of the United Church of Christ, the largest Protestant denomination in Japan. That such a small building—1,215 square feet (113 sq. m)—would cement Ando's reputation and influence architects following him is somewhat of a miracle; the budget was so limited that at one point the architect proposed leaving off the roof (the contractor eventually donated it), and the pews and floor were made from scaffolding planks, darkened to accentuate the light entering through the cross-shaped window behind the altar. From the exterior the effect of the cross of light is inversed; the window reads as dark lines against the gray concrete walls facing the street intersection of the low-scale residential neighborhood. The church is reached by a circuitous route that involves walking around the building, entering the church alongside an angled wall piercing its simple boxy form, and veering left and then right to encounter, finally, the room with the glowing cross.

Ten years after the April 1989 completion of the Church of the Light, Ando designed a replacement for the Sunday school, which includes an assembly hall, library, and kitchen housed in another exquisite concrete box. Almost the same size as the church, the school is placed next to it at an angle, connected by a curved canopy; a small courtyard with curved benches occupies the acute space between the two volumes. The church is open to visitors, but only on scheduled visiting days and only with a reservation. This sounds extreme for a petite church, but it is testament to the popularity of the design and the power of its draw.

1990 STADELHOFEN STATION

Santiago Calatrava ▸ Zürich, Switzerland

Station platforms looking southeast. The grid of pavers running alongside the track brings light to the subterranean concourse below the platform level.

Detail of concrete structure in the below-grade concourse. Calatrava's signature skeletal structure is illuminated by the pavers at the platform level above.

Initially gaining recognition for elegant suspension and cable-stayed bridges in his native Valencia and elsewhere in Spain, architect, artist, and engineer Santiago Calatrava (1951–) eventually became known for large, skeletal, and birdlike buildings with enormous budgets and extensive time lines, whose white surfaces stand in high relief from their urban contexts, whether Milwaukee, New York, or Santa Cruz de Tenerife (in Valencia he was given such a large canvas for the City of Arts and Sciences that his multiple buildings *are* the context). With such large projects, and their often accompanying controversy, his intervention for the Stadelhofen Station in the center of Zürich refreshingly integrates itself into its context, all the while exhibiting the structural sophistication in concrete and steel that are the hallmarks of Calatrava's subsequent projects.

Working with architect Arnold Amsler and landscape architect Werner Ruegger, Calatrava won a 1983 competition—his first—to rework and add a third track to an existing station in Zürich that serves as a node in the canton's regional rail network. The station is sited between Stadelhoferplatz and the Zürich Opera House on the west, and the Hohe Promenade hill—site of the city's old fortifications—on the east, the side where the third track was added. In lieu of a costlier and more time-consuming tunnel, Calatrava's winning design proposed excavating part of the hill and rebuilding a portion of it on concrete box beams held up by leaning, Y-shaped steel columns. These columns also support an elevated walkway that is capped by a trellis for plants from the reconstructed hillside. The platform between the new track and the second track is covered by the curved underside of the walkway, while commuters on the platform next to the first track (the farthest from the hillside) are covered by a translucent glass canopy. Glass blocks set into the platforms bring natural light to a subterranean retail concourse that is framed in shallow, riblike concrete arches.

Calatrava describes the design as "design by section," with the cross section of the three levels and the structural pieces defining them repeating along the curved path of the 885-foot-long (270 m) station. Breaking up the section are three bridges that bring people to the station from the hill above, while also connecting the areas east and west of the station. In effect these bridges stitch the city together across the curving tracks that cut across central Zürich.

1991 SAINSBURY WING, NATIONAL GALLERY

Robert Venturi, Denise Scott Brown and Associates ▸ London, England

The main stairway in the new wing. Behind the new wing's modern glass is a grand stair that ascends from the entrance off the square to the galleries two floors up.

The new wing seen from Trafalgar Square. The playful repetition of columns is evident in the facade of the addition at left, but so are modern touches: a glass wall facing it and skylights above the top-floor galleries.

In 1984, just when it seemed that London was going to receive a modern addition to the National Gallery designed by William Wilkins in the 1830s, the Prince of Wales opened his mouth and squashed the project, eventually leading to the postmodern design of husband-and-wife architects Robert Venturi (1925–) and Denise Scott Brown (1931–). At a celebration of the 150th anniversary of the Royal Institute of British Architects (RIBA), His Royal Highness famously described the original competition's winning design as "a monstrous carbuncle on the face of a much loved and elegant friend." Although the words carry a small bit of irony (Wilkins's design was often derided on aesthetic and functional grounds and renovated piecemeal like a stone Frankenstein's monster), the prince's less-quoted words that followed portend the building that his mum, Queen Elizabeth II, would open on July 9, 1991: "It defeats me why anyone wishing to display the Early Renaissance pictures belonging to the Gallery should do so in a new gallery so manifestly at odds with the whole spirit of that age."

Prince Charles wasn't the only person responsible for the shift to a much different design. Brothers John, Simon, and Timothy Sainsbury, heirs to the eponymous supermarket chain, pledged to cover the costs of the 120,000 square-foot (11,000 sq. m) wing, meaning the office component, an integral part of the "carbuncle" scheme, would be unnecessary. Freed from financial stress, the gallery held a closed competition and unanimously selected Venturi and Scott Brown's reserved design that explicitly respects the Wilkins building, the adjacent Trafalgar Square, and the Renaissance art that would hang on its walls.

Outside, the Sainsbury Wing matches the Portland stone of the original edifice, replicating its Corinthian pilasters but playing with them in a Mannerist fashion—the pilaster farthest from the Wilkins building almost detaches itself from the curving facade, echoing Nelson's Column in the middle of Trafalgar Square, while columns with Egyptian motifs are also present. The exterior isn't free from modern touches: a glass curtain wall faces the west side of the Wilkins building across a narrow walkway. Behind this glass wall is a grand stairway that ascends two floors from the entrance to the new galleries and acts as a link to the main building's galleries. Inspired by visits to Italian galleries with the client, Venturi and Scott Brown designed galleries with high natural light brought in by a system of skylights and lanterns, arched openings—some with contemporary Tuscan columns—connecting the enfilade of rooms, and the use of stone and stucco throughout. The paintings are at home in the galleries, just as the addition is at home in the center of London.

1992 KUNSTHAL

Office for Metropolitan Architecture ▸ Rotterdam, Netherlands

Inside the auditorium. The leaning columns (one of them is visible below the tower in the exterior photo) were one of the touches that brought immediate attention to the Kunsthal when it opened in 1992.

The building seen from the south. The road cutting through the building, as well as steps up to the busy road atop a dike, can be seen at right.

Even before he realized a single building, Dutch architect Rem Koolhaas (1944–) was a household name thanks to *Delirious New York: A Retroactive Manifesto for Manhattan*, published in 1978, three years before he cofounded the Office for Metropolitan Architecture (OMA). His thoroughly original analysis of the city's "culture of congestion" ushered in a fresh voice in architecture that would someday make its mark on cities around the world. That someday came on the first day of November 1992, when the Kunsthal opened in his native city's Museumpark.

The Museumpark is a small swath of land between the nineteenth-century Museum Boijmans Van Beuningen, a World War II survivor, and the Erasmus MC, a university medical complex with modern facades designed by Jean Prouvé. The Kunsthal, which contains exhibition spaces, an auditorium, and a café, is located on the park's southern edge, alongside the busy east-west Westzeedijk that runs atop a dike. On the northern edge of the park is the Het Nieuwe Instituut, formerly the Netherlands Architecture Institute designed by Jo Coenen. In between the two contemporary buildings are a parade ground and a garden that Koolhaas designed with landscape architect Yves Brunier.

The Kunsthal bridges a frontage road parallel to the highway, and one story up it is pierced by a ramp running north-south that turns the building into a gateway to the park. The ramp divides the square-plan building into two sides, which Koolhaas and company at OMA connected by a complex series of stairs, ramps, and walkways that proceed through the exhibition and other spaces in a roughly counterclockwise spiral. The interlocking of spaces in section, the mix of expensive and cheap materials, and the irreverent form-making found in the Kunsthal would become signatures of later Koolhaas buildings on a much larger scale, such as in the Seattle Central Library (2004) and the CCTV Headquarters (see 2012).

The Kunsthal was established as a venue for temporary blockbuster exhibitions, and one of them would prove history making. In the early morning of October 16, 2012, two thieves stole seven paintings—a Picasso, a Matisse, and two Monets among them—from a twentieth-anniversary show. This scandalous event, along with the changing nature of government funding in the Netherlands, among other reasons, led to a renovation of the Kunsthal by OMA, completed in 2014. They overhauled the museum's previously lackluster security, improved the building's thermal performance through new glazing and mechanical systems, reoriented the entry sequence, and separated the once flowing spaces in concert with the mechanical improvements, allowing different exhibitions and events to be held simultaneously. Thankfully, the last was done with glass partitions, so the complex sectional adjacencies of the original design are visually maintained.

1993 VITRA FIRE STATION

Zaha Hadid Architects ▸ Weil am Rhein, Germany

The fire station seen from the east. This design's dynamism is expressed most dramatically in the tapered canopy supported by a bundle of upright and slender leaning steel *pilotis*.

Sometimes the worst situations lead to the most positive outcomes. In 1981, the Swiss company Vitra, which has been manufacturing designer furniture since 1950, lost half of its production facilities in Weil am Rhein to a fire. Rolf Fehlbaum, who had just taken over management of the company from his parents, saw an opportunity to hire well-known young architects to create a campus with architecturally distinguished buildings to parallel the company's output of furnishings designed by Charles and Ray Eames, Jean Prouvé, George Nelson, and others.

At the center of the campus, fittingly, is the fire station, the first completed building of Iraqi-born, London-based architect Zaha Hadid (1950–2016). Before its completion in 1993, Vitra realized two factory buildings designed by British architect Nicholas Grimshaw (who is responsible for the master plan of the Vitra campus), three buildings designed by Frank Gehry, most notably the Vitra Design Museum (1989), and a conference pavilion designed by Japanese architect Tadao Ando, completed the same year as the fire station. Subsequent additions to the campus include factory buildings designed by Portuguese architect Álvaro Siza (1994) and Japan's SANAA (2012), and Herzog & de Meuron's VitraHaus (2010), a large building with stacked gable forms where Vitra displays its wares to the public.

Hadid's fire station is positioned between factory buildings along the campus's main east-west axis, meaning a repeat of the 1981 fire wouldn't occur. (Viewed from the public areas on the eastern edge of campus, the fire station is framed fortuitously by the bridgelike canopy Siza designed as a covered passage between production facilities.) Inspired by the vineyards and agricultural fields that lie just beyond the campus, Hadid designed the concrete-and-glass building as an extension of those patterns in the landscape, an inversion of the Peak—an unrealized, competition-winning project from 1982 that brought her international attention and a spot in MoMA's 1988 *Deconstructivist Architecture* show with fellow Vitra architect Frank Gehry, in which the skyscrapers of Hong Kong were abstracted into barlike forms and inserted horizontally into the hillside above the city. At Weil am Rhein, nature, manicured as it is, is the impetus, and it is fashioned into layered spaces between angular walls that seem caught in the act of exploding.

After only a few years, the fire station ceased operating. Detractors of Hadid's aggressive, Constructivist-derived form chalked the closure up to the unsuitability of the building's narrow, elongated spaces for storing fire trucks. The reality was that the Vitra campus didn't need its own brigade after the surrounding town added nearby facilities. Now the building is used for exhibitions and events.

1994 BOWALI VISITOR CENTRE

Glenn Murcutt and Troppo Architects ▸ Kakadu National Park, Australia

Looking south along the veranda. Rammed-earth construction, which accompanies the wood and metal, helps root the building into its site.

Aerial view looking north. The long building capped by metal roofs weaves its way into the Top End landscape.

Most of the buildings designed by Sydney architect Glenn Murcutt (1936–) are private dwellings scattered about New South Wales, Australia. Less than a handful of his (at least) dozens of buildings are open to the public, including the Moss Vale Education Centre (2007) at the University of Wollongong, carried out with Wendy Lewin; the limited-access Boyd Education Centre (1999, the venue of his famous annual "Master Class") at Riversdale, with Lewin and Reg Clark; and the Bowali Visitor Centre with Troppo Architects, the duo of Phil Harris and Adrian Welke. Such is the nature of Murcutt's one-man practice that he primarily carries out houses alone, and then teams up with other architects on larger jobs. Whatever the typology, his buildings have a sensitivity to place—climate, topography, and culture—that remains consistent.

The Bowali Visitor Centre, named for nearby Bowali Creek, is located 2,300 miles (3,700 km) northwest of Sydney in the Northern Territory's Kakadu National Park. This geographic remove from Australia's most populous city not only illustrates the vast scale of the country, it hints at the cultural and natural diversity to be found in the nearly 7,700 square-mile (20,000 sq. km–about half the size of Switzerland!) preserve that is about a three-hour drive east from Darwin. Owned and managed in part by the Aborigines who have lived in the area for more than fifty thousand years, the park features a great diversity of landscapes and wildlife, and is also home to exceptional Aboriginal rock art, earning the place UNESCO World Heritage status in 1981.

In 1987, Troppo Architects was hired to design a number of buildings in the park: rangers' housing, an entry station, ablution blocks, and a bird information center. Their use of corrugated metal, pitched roofs, water catchments, and other economically and environmentally responsive devices aligned them with Murcutt, whom they had met by chance in 1983. When it came time to compete for the Bowali Visitor Centre, Troppo teamed up with Murcutt and won the commission. Their design incorporated the Bird Information Centre and used it as a starting point for a linear building with various indoor spaces connected by a long veranda. This and other elements, such as a winglike roof with huge gutter, respond to the area's wide-ranging climate marked by monsoons, storms, humidity, cold weather, and dry, hot weather. Walking across the veranda, in and out of the different rooms, is akin to exploring the park, most notably in the use of rammed-earth walls that echo the Aboriginal caves where much of their rock art is found.

1995 KANDALAMA HOTEL

Geoffrey Bawa ▸ Dambulla, Sri Lanka

The view from terrace to terrace. Built into an existing slope, Bawa's design gives all of the hotel rooms dramatic views of the surrounding landscape.

Sri Lankan architect Geoffrey Bawa (1919–2003) designed and realized many hotels in his long career, but a good number of them were clustered in the 1990s, following the defeat of the People's Liberation Front in 1989 and the subsequent lull in the violence that had plagued the country for nearly a decade. One of these hotels was commissioned by Aitken Spence, which had hired Bawa in the late 1970s for the Triton Hotel in Ahungalla on the country's west coast, in what is known as its Wet Zone. Kandalama Hotel (now Heritance Kandalama) would be the inverse of Triton Hotel (now Heritance Ahungalla): situated inland in Sri Lanka's Dry Zone, designed with flat roofs instead of Bawa's typical pitched roofs, and embedding itself within the landscape so deeply that sometimes it is hard to distinguish the two.

The impetus for the hotel's inland position is the fifth-century ruins of Sigiriya and its 600-foot-high (180 m) Lion Rock, which dominates the jungle from all directions. Aware of its presence, Bawa turned down the nearby site the hotelier had an option on and instead selected a site at a remove from the ancient city, along a distant ridge on the edge of Kandalama reservoir. He designed the hotel so visitors approach the hotel through the jungle, encounter the hotel built into the rocky landscape, and move through its cavelike corridors to the terraces that look onto the water and Sigiriya beyond. Every room—sleeping rooms, spas, restaurants, even toilet rooms—look out onto the terraces and the amazing views. Although he was forced to modify his plans in response to concerns of monks from a nearby temple and environmentalists concerned about the hotel's effect on the reservoir, the idea of a hotel hidden in the jungle and laden with mystery remains.

The biggest departure from Bawa's earlier projects such as the Triton Hotel was not just the flat roofs; rather, it was the decision to employ an external concrete frame to support the terraces and timber sunscreens; vegetation clings to the latter to cover the building from the ground to the roof gardens. Given that Bawa's design was realized with the most minimal means of intrusion on the landscape (no earth-moving machines were used, and rock formations were maintained and incorporated into the design), it's fitting that the hotel has become part of the landscape, a place from which to appreciate the surroundings.

1996 THERME VALS

Peter Zumthor ▸ Vals, Switzerland

The central pool with skylights. The linear gaps between the cantilevered concrete roofs cast streaks of light down the walls covered in gneiss stone.

Therme Vals seen from the east. Set into a slope next to the hotel, the two-story spa looks like a smooth stone mass with carved openings.

From September 1995 to January 1996, the Museum of Modern Art (MoMA) in New York held the exhibition *Light Construction*, highlighting projects that fit into what curator Terence Riley called "a new architecture of transparency and translucency." One of the projects was the Kunsthaus Bregenz (1997) in Austria by Peter Zumthor (1943–), a box covered in translucent glass panes that overlap like shingles, with galleries illuminated by glass ceilings. Zumthor's contribution stands as an anomaly in a diverse oeuvre of otherwise solid, heavy projects—the antithesis of lightness. The spa he designed for the Therme Vals hotel and bath complex in Switzerland's Graubünden canton is the most famous example of this alternative to what was, according to MoMA, a prevalent architectural trend at the time.

Zumthor's design replaced the hotel's existing spa, making it the third one on the spot in Vals, a small town in the narrow Valser Rhine river valley that is blessed with a warm-water spring. Instead of designing a building that fit aesthetically with the admittedly 1960s-looking hotel, Zumthor opted for something that would look older than its neighbor, older still than the original nineteenth-century spa. He described his design "of always having been in the landscape," and from the hotel it literally disappears below a green roof. To achieve this intention on the inside as well he built the spa entirely *from* the surrounding landscape, specifically a gneiss stone quarried just up the valley.

Access to the spa is from the hotel, through an underground tunnel that readies the mind and body for the cavelike sensation of the baths. Zumthor designed them as a number of blocks that bathers move among in a casual manner, without any set order. The blocks appear monolithic but are in fact hollow, made of concrete walls covered in thin layers of the dark gneiss stone and containing baths with waters of different temperatures, uses, and even fragrances. Each block is capped by a cantilevered concrete roof that stops just short of its neighbor. The narrow, glass-filled gaps bring daylight to the otherwise dark spaces, often through dramatic streaks cast across the walls. Most memorable is a central pool that sits between four of the blocks under a grid of sixteen small square skylights, matched in scale by an exterior pool that can be reached by the stone deck or via a connected indoor pool. While the valley that Therme Vals sits in is framed by large windows inside the spa, outside those views come with a roof of blue, a light counterpoint to the primordial baths.

1997 GUGGENHEIM MUSEUM BILBAO

Frank Gehry ▸ **Bilbao, Spain**

Looking up at the atrium. This vertical center of the museum is a confusing space of different surfaces and materials, but a fitting canvas for an Ernesto Neto installation.

The museum seen from the northwest. The Guggenheim's choice to build on the edge of the river gives the institution high visibility.

Without a doubt the Guggenheim Museum Bilbao has had the greatest impact on the course of contemporary architecture in the past twenty years. Its opening on the banks of the Nervión river brought an immense amount of attention to Frank Gehry (1929–), to Bilbao, and to architecture in general. Although the Basque Country Administration invested in much more than just the Guggenheim (a new airport terminal and pedestrian bridge over the Nervión designed by Santiago Calatrava and a subway system designed by Norman Foster, to name a few), Gehry and his museum are often credited with single-handedly reversing the city's industrial decline and transforming it into a cultural magnet—the now famous "Bilbao effect." The museum attracted two million visitors in its first year of operation, heralding a wave of cultural buildings around the world hoping for similar success. Furthermore, the building influenced architects through its bold forms, striking titanium cladding, and incorporation of innovative computer technologies.

Even before he won the invited competition in 1991, Gehry had visited the city with Solomon R. Guggenheim Foundation director Thomas Krens earlier that year, when they had determined that a riverfront site would be preferable to the ornate, former wine-storage building that the city wanted to renovate. The site on the south bank of the Nervión dictated much of Gehry's design, especially how it would look from the north bank of the river and how the form would skirt under La Salve Bridge and culminate in a tower—the tail of the fishlike building. Squared off and covered in stone to the south where it meets the city through a plaza that bridges over a roadway, the building is all titanium-clad ripples, folds, and pinches toward the river, where it rises to a climax roughly the same height as the tower.

Comparisons with Frank Lloyd Wright's Solomon R. Guggenheim Museum (see 1959) in New York are inevitable, as Wright's building also imposes its will on its surroundings (and the artists on display) through unique and unprecedented form-making; sits on an edge, with the city on one side and a natural feature opposite (a park in New York, a river in Bilbao), providing, if not forcing, a frontal view; and is oriented about a large atrium. In this last case the spiral form of Wright's atrium can be grasped both outside and inside, but Gehry's atrium is a disorienting assemblage of glass, plaster, and stone rising to skylights and traversed by walkways. Differences aside, they are both self-referential designs that put their own architecture on display as much as the art they contain.

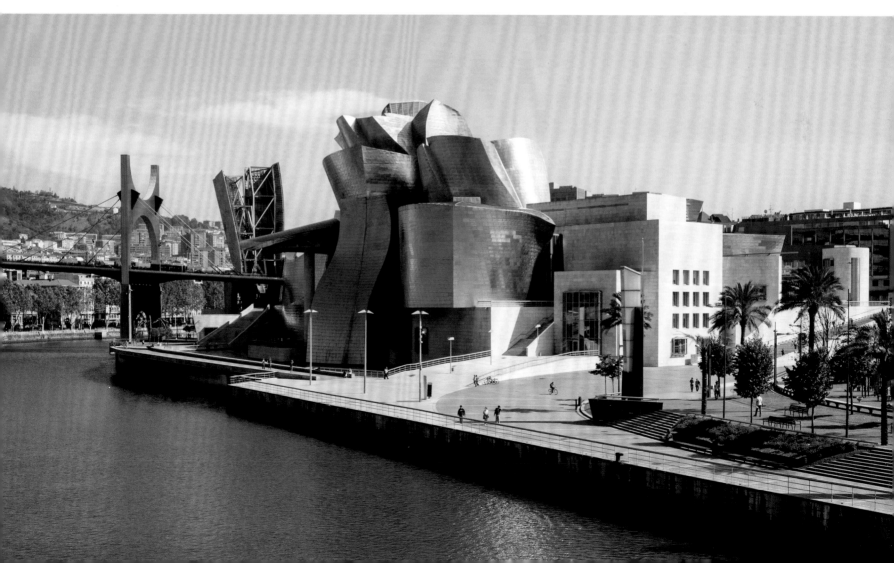

1998 TJIBAOU CULTURAL CENTRE

Renzo Piano Building Workshop ▸ Nouméa, New Caledonia

The cultural center seen from the south. Piano arrayed the cases along a curved east-west spine that overlooks a lagoon to the north.

Detail of wood case. With its operable louvers and convection chimneys, the building supposedly ventilates itself as effectively during hot and humid days as it does during the periodic monsoons.

The last of French President François Mitterrand's *Grands Projets* to be realized is also the only one outside of Paris—the Tjibaou Cultural Centre, located on an island of New Caledonia near New Zealand. Through its remote setting and its synthesis of local culture and contemporary technology, the design by Renzo Piano (1937–) is arguably the most exceptional of the *Grands Projets*.

Mitterrand decided to build a cultural center on New Caledonia, a French territory since the mid 1800s, that would conserve as well as promote the advancement of the dwindling indigenous Kanak culture. The building takes its name from Jean-Marie Tjibaou, the Kanak leader who negotiated the 1988 Matignon Accords in their struggle to gain independence from France; the accords were only a partial victory and one year later Tjibaou was assassinated by a fellow Kanak. A competition was held in 1991 for the building that would also honor his memory, and Renzo Piano Building Workshop won with a design based on the tepeelike huts of the Kanaks.

If the cultural center had been built according to Piano's winning design, it would not be as cherished a building as it is today, since it was overly literal, bordering on mimicry. Thankfully, the Italian architect developed the design away from the literal vernacular form and toward a wholly unique form rooted in a strategy of natural ventilation. Each of the ten "cases" (as Piano calls his version of the Kanak huts) is made from two layers of laminated Iroko wood ribs whose gaps create a natural convection chimney controlled by operable louvers. The cases contain Kanak sculptures, lecture halls, a classroom, a library, and a café, while a one-story, flat-roofed portion connects the cases along a circulation spine and adds gallery space, offices, services, and an auditorium.

In addition to the cases, the site planning integrates the building into its locale in three ways. First, Piano chose a peninsula site between the sea to the south and a lagoon to the north that was an existing bare patch among the trees, in an effort to minimize the disturbance of the vegetation. Second, he oriented the cases to the south and the flat-roofed portion to the north so the trade winds would work with the cases' convection chimneys. And third, Piano worked with an ethnologist to develop, among other things, the pedestrian approach to the building to parallel the Kanak tradition where the chief is positioned at the head and others arrive in the middle. Therefore visitors to the Tjibaou Cultural Centre arrive in the middle of the building rather than at its end, to venture across the building to learn about the culture that inspired the design.

1999 JEWISH MUSEUM BERLIN

Daniel Libeskind ▸ Berlin, Germany

Inside one of the museum's voids. Libeskind confronts the horror of the Holocaust most effectively in the mute and hollow voids that cut across the zigzag plan.

Aerial view of the museum from the east. Libeskind's angular and aggressive building is a sharp contrast from the Collegienhaus, whose courtyard Libeskind covered with glass in 2007.

Two years before its official opening in the fall of 2001, the Jewish Museum Berlin opened as an empty shell, inviting 350,000 visitors to move through the haunting spaces designed by Daniel Libeskind (1946–) ten years earlier. The popularity of the building in those two years is a testament to the power of Libeskind's daring, unprecedented design, as well as its extra-long period of fruition, stemming more from political and bureaucratic foibles than architectural design.

A lot changed in those dozen years. Only seven months after the competition results were announced in early 1989, the Berlin Wall came down. Before Libeskind was named the winner of what was planned as a 165,000 square-foot (15,300 sq. m) extension of the Berlin Museum (it became an independent museum upon its opening), he had built only installations. The same month the museum opened in 2001, terrorists brought down the Twin Towers in New York; in the following year Libeskind would design the winning master plan for the World Trade Center.

Trained at Cooper Union in New York, Libeskind was known in the 1970s and 1980s as a professor and "paper architect." In hindsight, his earlier drawings and project proposals made him an obvious choice for articulating the senseless destruction and loss of life that World War II and the Holocaust inflicted on Jews. No Modern or postmodern design would suffice; something alien and free of associations needed to be realized in the place where the violence originated. Libeskind achieved this with a zigzag plan generated by complex lines that are alternately an exploded Star of David and a connect-the-dots map of Holocaust survivors living in the area of the museum's Friedrichstadt neighborhood. Diagonal gouges in the zinc facade capture a feeling of violence, even as the post-2001 exhibits inside cover up those openings.

The greatest power of the Jewish Museum Berlin is found in the "voids" and other spaces that exist outside of the galleries. They start inside the eighteenth-century Collegienhaus, where a concrete core pierces a corner of the Baroque building and leads visitors to the basement level. From here a narrow walkway leads to a stairway in Libeskind's building pierced by diagonal concrete beams. Cutting across the zigzag plan parallel to the Collegienhaus are windowless, skylighted voids that are inaccessible, except in one instance where the floor is covered in metallic disks that echo when stepped on. The inverse of one void is built as a concrete tower outside the museum, giving visitors an escape to the Garden of Exile and Emigration, where life in the form of vegetation atop a grid of leaning columns is visible but just out of reach.

2000 SENDAI MEDIATHEQUE

Toyo Ito ▸ Sendai, Japan

Interior seen along the south-facing wall. Some of the bundled tubes are open to visually connect floors, while others are enclosed to house vertical circulation and even mechanical services.

The south elevation. The building faces a wide, tree-lined boulevard on the south, from where it displays the bundled tubes it is known for.

Although the prevalence of information stored in digital formats points to the death of libraries, it has also reinforced the role of libraries as social spaces. The digital revolution combined with millennium fever in the late 1990s led to reconsiderations of what a library should be, and the Sendai Mediatheque—a two-and-a-half-hour bullet train ride north from Tokyo—is one of the most famous, and most architecturally ambitious, examples.

Sendai Mediatheque was conceived in 1995 as a combination of traditional library, library for people with vision and hearing impairments, gallery, and audiovisual learning center. Toyo Ito's (1941–) winning design concept was based on freedom and breaking down the walls of traditional rooms to allow the users of a building the ability to shape the building in their own ways over time. Sure, the completed building has walls for the necessities of any building (bathrooms, for instance), but from the beginning the design was simply floor upon floor of open space flowing around columns of bundled tubes, all behind glass walls with horizontal patterns. An early competition model expressed only these three parts—floors, structure, skin—such that the columns of bundled tubes resembled seaweed floating underwater; it was a dramatic image only marginally suited to the building's purpose, but it prevailed until well after the building was completed in August 2000 (the library moved in four months later and the building opened to the public in January the following year).

As much an ambitious expression of contemporary architecture and an innovative program for twenty-first-century learning and culture, the building is also a daring feat of structural engineering. Ito worked with engineer Mutsuro Sasaki to turn his concept of thirteen twisted and angled seaweedlike columns of varying diameters and uses into a built reality. Their collaborative skill in designing and engineering the building for earthquake-prone Japan was put to the test in 2011 during the horrific 9.0 magnitude quake whose epicenter was only 80 miles (129 km) east of Sendai. A viral video posted online by a patron who took shelter below a table for a frightening three minutes showed furniture sliding about the floors and the ceiling moving back and forth independently of the tubes. Some glass broke and a section of ceiling fell, but the building was otherwise unscathed, showing that earthquake-resistant buildings can take many forms.

2001 EDEN PROJECT

Nicholas Grimshaw ▸ Cornwall, England

Inside the Biomes. The two Biomes—Humid Tropics Biome and Warm Temperate Biome—are made up of eight linked geodesic domes.

The Biomes seen from the south. The Biomes are wonderfully odd structures, signs of optimism in a postindustrial landscape.

Even before it officially opened to the public on Easter Sunday 2001, nearly a half-million people had visited the Eden Project to see it take shape. In anticipation of these large numbers, a visitor center was built in 2000, followed by the two Biomes in 2001. As the name implies, work on the buildings and the remediated landscape they are built into is ongoing, paralleling the natural processes that Eden embraces. Regardless, most of the attention has been given, appropriately, to the Biomes, which are also the focus here.

The Eden Project was built under the United Kingdom's Millennium Commission, which from 1993 to 2006 used lottery funds to realize buildings, events, and other projects celebrating the turn of the second millennium. The most famous and controversial of the projects was the Millennium Dome in London, but many of the projects were built outside the national capital. The decision to build in southwest England can be attributed primarily to Tim Smit, a former music producer who restored the Lost Gardens of Heligan after moving to Cornwall in the mid-1980s. Those gardens served as a pilot project for the Eden Project, which Smit envisioned as a symbol of optimism that would transform a derelict clay-mining pit into a place to study plants, our interaction with nature, and the application of science toward the stewardship of the earth in the twenty-first century.

Smit hired Nicholas Grimshaw (1939–) based on his design of the International Terminal Waterloo (1993) in London. That project served as the starting point for what would become the Biomes: the architect took the same curved profile of the terminal's glass roof and applied it to one side of a cliff on the site, like a leaning greenhouse. Almost immediately that scheme was deemed too costly, eventually leading to the use of triple-layer, air-filled ETFE (ethylene tetrafluoroethylene, a plastic with good thermal performance) foil "pillows" set into hexagonal frames and arranged like a series of soap bubbles across the postindustrial landscape. Linked by a low, grass-covered entrance, the two Biomes follow the initial approach, in that the spheres lean against the cliffs to immerse visitors in the horticultural realms contained by the naturally ventilated domes.

Resembling the lovechild of Bucky Fuller's geodesic domes and the soap bubble research of Frei Otto, the Eden Project's ETFE Biomes pioneered the material's wider application. Subsequent buildings wrapped in ETFE include the Allianz Arena (2005) in Munich by Herzog & de Meuron and the National Aquatics Center (2008) in Beijing by PTW Architects.

2002 BIBLIOTHECA ALEXANDRINA

Snøhetta ▸ Alexandria, Egypt

The reading room. Held up by round concrete columns, the roof is structured as a technologically complex screen with solar sails to diffuse light.

The exterior seen from the southwest. The inclined wall is covered in stone bands carved with characters from extinct symbolic languages—e.g., cuneiform and hieroglyphics—and patterns from nature.

When the Bibliotheca Alexandrina was completed in fall 2001, it launched a yearlong inauguration that culminated with the official opening of the library in October 2002. While a year is a long time to celebrate a contemporary building, it is a mere flash within the library's entire existence, which reaches back to ancient Egypt and should extend far into the future. In fact, the design by Norway's Snøhetta—founded by Craig Dykers (1961–) and Kjetil Trædal Thorsen (1958–) two years before they won the library's 1989 competition—incorporates time as an important element of its symbolism and meaning.

The Ancient Library of Alexandria, built more than 2,300 years ago, marked a dramatic change in human history. It was there that Euclid discovered the elements of geometry; Herophilos established the rules of anatomy; and Ptolemy and Eratosthenes used science to measure and describe the world. Home to the largest collection of text in the world at the time, the "Great Library" was supposedly destroyed by Julius Caesar during the Roman Civil War in 48 BCE and rebuilt multiple times since.

Well aware of this history, Snøhetta designed a building that looks like it could stand for a thousand years. Embedded with symbolism throughout, the 525-foot-diameter (160 m) building inclines toward the Mediterranean Sea on the north and cuts into the ground as a voyage back in time; this historical excavation finds its parallel inside the reading room. At the south end of the building is a tall inclined wall carved with dead languages, the high point of the microchip-like roof over the reading room; the future is propped up by the layers of history literally written upon the surfaces of the walls.

Even without an awareness of this intended symbolism on the part of the architects, visitors to the Aga Khan Award–winning Bibliotheca Alexandrina can appreciate the architecture of the new library and its importance in the city and in Egypt. Below the angled glass roof sits the impressive reading room, seven tiered floors that recede into the earth yet maintain a connection to the sky. Outside of the library functions, the Bibliotheca Alexandrina houses a planetarium, several museums, a school for information science, and conservation facilities, which makes it an important cultural spot in the city. It's no wonder that in early 2011, when unrest swept through Egypt, a makeshift group of young people occupied the plaza to protect the library from looters and vandals so it can survive longer than its predecessors.

2003 SELFRIDGES

Future Systems ▸ Birmingham, England

The department store seen from the east. Selfridges occupies the easternmost portion of the Bullring Shopping Centre overlooking a neighboring church as a study in contrasts.

When Vittorio Radice asked Jan Kaplický (1937–2009) if his new store anchoring the Bullring Shopping Centre in Birmingham would need a sign, the architect replied it would not be necessary. Although signage now adorns some of the street-level windows, it's clear from Kaplický's response that the building should be more than enough advertising for the UK department store. In a way the client's question was a bit of a ruse—why hire Future Systems, the firm that added a spaceshiplike media center to Lord's Cricket Ground and proposed an office building that resembled a strawberry for Trafalgar Square, if recognition was not the intended result?

If Kaplický and Amanda Levete (1955–), his partner at Future Systems and in life at the time, had initially had their way, the four-story building would have been wrapped in glass walls to highlight the movement of shoppers inside. But with the retailer's desire for more display space and fewer distractions for shoppers, the store went in the opposite direction and became almost entirely solid. In a concerted effort to create a landmark in an area devoid of architectural personality—including the rest of the Bullring complex (minus the appealing nineteenth-century church next door)—the duo found inspiration in a Paco Rabanne dress and covered the 270,000 square-foot (25,000 sq. m) steel-framed building with 15,000 anodized aluminum discs bolted to the curvaceous concrete shell. Backed by a blue surface, the discs shimmer in the daylight and stand out at night thanks to integral lighting. Blob-shaped openings, appropriate given the store's form, pierce the otherwise consistent, scaleless wrapper in a few spots to connect inside and outside, most memorably in a curling bridge from a parking garage across the street.

Although not as striking or memorable as the exterior, a full-height, skylighted atrium lined with glossy white surfaces and crisscrossed by escalators brings natural light to the three floors of fashion and the food hall on the ground floor, popular since the store opened on September 4, 2003.

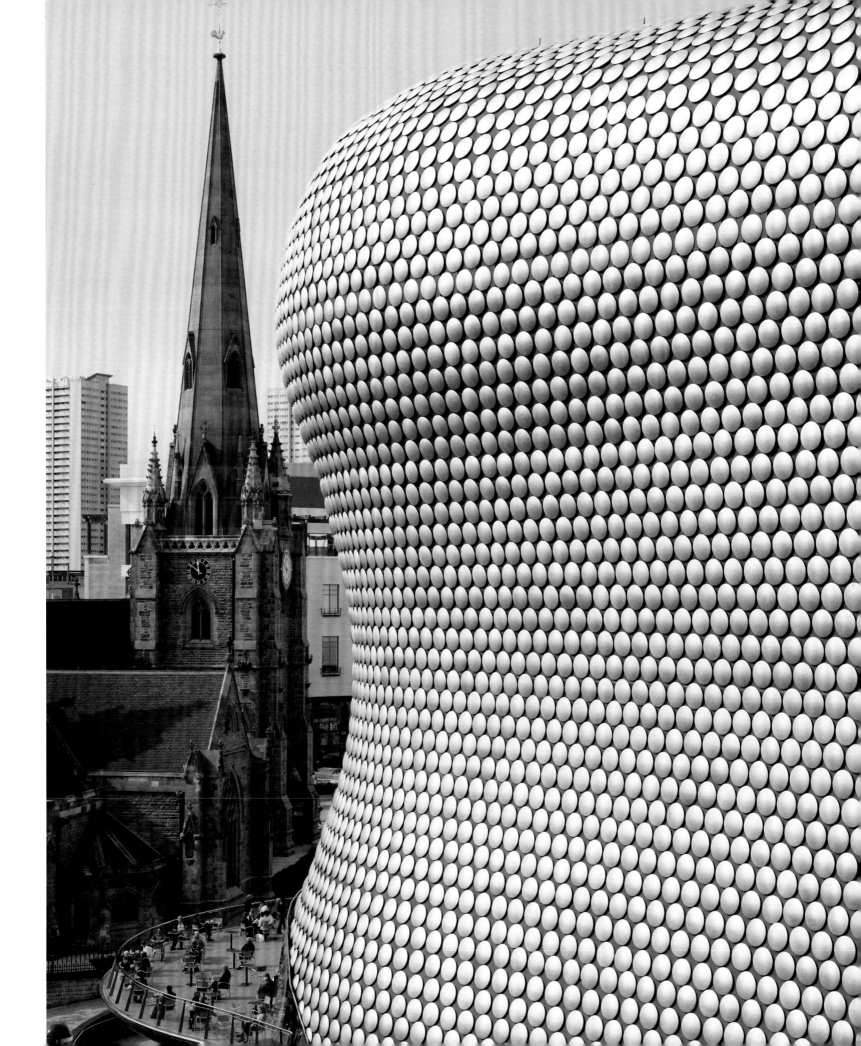

2004 THE SCOTTISH PARLIAMENT

Enric Miralles and Benedetta Tagliabue ▸ Edinburgh, Scotland

Inside the Debating Chamber. The complexity extends to the wood structure over the main democratic space of the Scottish Parliament, where visitors can watch government in action.

The northeast corner of the Scottish Parliament. Although highly complex and expressive, the building features a number of recurring motifs, including the L-shaped panels that overlap the windows.

Catalan architect Enric Miralles (1955–2000) had a highly mature yet playful signature expression that brought him much attention and commissions. Yet almost as quickly as he garnered fame, he fell victim to a brain tumor at the age of only forty-five, about two years into his and his second wife and partner Benedetta Tagliabue's (1963–) most important project. It would be another four years before the Scottish Parliament opened for government business on October 9, 2004—four years of delays, cost overruns, political squabbles, and bad publicity that soured the ambitious design and the architect's legacy. But not long after the building was completed and visited by hundreds of thousands of people, it was proclaimed a masterpiece. Like Louis I. Kahn's National Assembly Building in Dhaka, Bangladesh (see 1983), the Scottish Parliament is a gift of democracy to one country from an architect from another.

The project began in January 1998—four months after the devolution referendum that would lead to the Scottish Parliament—when Holyrood, at the foot of the Royal Mile east of Edinburgh's city center, was selected as the site of the future parliament building. A three-stage competition was held shortly thereafter, with the firm of Miralles and Tagliabue (EMBT), in partnership with the large Edinburgh practice RMJM, chosen in July of that year. Instrumental in the selection and evolution of the project was Donald Dewar, the inaugural first minister of Scotland. Like Miralles, Dewar died in 2000, never to see the building completed. His enthusiastic embrace of the architect's somewhat oppositional ideas of parliament's "growing out of the land" and not being a building at all (it is, as stated in EMBT's competition entry, "a mental place") was instrumental in the design's selection and path toward realization.

At its most basic, the sizable Scottish Parliament is an L-shaped plan with spaces that radiate out from its entrance at the northeast. But Holyrood, as it is also known, is far from basic. It consists of at least five distinct yet interconnected buildings within the larger building: the sculpted concrete of the Canongate Buildings and the neighboring renovation of Queensberry House, the layered four-story facade signaling the individual offices of the MSPs (members of the Scottish Parliament), the Tower Buildings that recall upturned boats, and the "concrete branches" reaching out into the landscape. A few steps into the parliament building reveals the Kemnay granite and Caithness stone used throughout, but the clear focus is the Debating Chamber, a petal-shaped space of wood, steel, and glass. The MSP's desks and the gallery's chairs designed by Enric Miralles are but two illustrations of the level of detail he achieved in this grandest expression of his architectural talent.

2005 DE YOUNG MUSEUM

Herzog & de Meuron ▸ San Francisco, California, United States

Looking south from the tower. The view from the level 9 observation deck is panoramic, including another addition to the park: Renzo Piano's California Academy of Sciences.

The museum seen from the southeast. The shaded overhang on the long elevation subtly indicates the main entrance through a courtyard cut into the building's rectangular plan.

Every place has its defining natural characteristics, the landscapes that temper our experiences, sink into our memories and, in the context of this book, give architects inspiration. San Francisco is a city blessed with amazing beauty in its hills, trees, beaches, and waterways, but the natural feature that defines it most is invisible, underground, and evident when least expected: earthquakes. My first visit to the city happened to coincide with an earthquake centered in Napa Valley, which derailed a planned trip to wine country but more important has stuck with me since as *the* strongest memory of that visit. Even for people who have not felt the ground shake when there, San Francisco is forever associated with earthquakes.

So it's not surprising that the de Young Museum, located in Golden Gate Park, looks like a building fissured by seismic activity, a built illustration of the forces out of sight but all too real. That the museum appears to be seismically influenced, intentionally or not, is also not surprising given that the building's predecessor was the victim of two major earthquakes. In 1906—eleven years after it opened as the Memorial Museum—the Fine Arts Building was seriously damaged in the April 18 earthquake that, with resulting fires, destroyed most of the city by the bay. Then in 1989, the Loma Prieta earthquake struck, but this time damages were irreparable; the building—then much larger and housing the M. H. de Young Memorial Museum and the Asian Art Museum (the latter moved near the San Francisco Civic Center in 2003)—had to come down.

It would take ten years for an architect to be selected—the Swiss firm of Jacques Herzog (1950–) and Pierre de Meuron (1950–)—following struggles with an architecturally conservative population that voted down two attempts to fund the museum through public money. With solely private funds and a nod from the city, the museum moved ahead finally in 2002 with Herzog & de Meuron's design, which they compared to continental shelves as well as fingers that unite park and museum. When it opened to the public on October 15, 2005, the museum stood out in its setting through a perforated copper skin, but over time the brown surfaces will patina to blend into the green surroundings. Generous glass walls, a large cantilevered roof (also covered in copper) on the south, and courtyards cut into the building invite people from the park to the museum. The low, two-story building is topped by a nine-story, 144-foot-tall (44 m) tower in the northwest corner that torques as it rises, a further reference to the city's seismic foundation.

2006 GLASS PAVILION, TOLEDO MUSEUM OF ART

SANAA ▸ Toledo, Ohio, United States

Inside the exhibition area. The two layers of glass walls create an interstitial zone with thermal and acoustic benefits, but they also add visual complexity to the whole experience.

The Glass Pavilion seen from the southeast. Some of the spaces in the almost all-glass building are outfitted with reflective curtains (visible in the middle of the photo) to cut down on heat infiltration.

Even if museums from the past one hundred years are highly controlled environments that use artificial lighting and indirect natural lighting to create the ideal conditions for curators to display art, there is something fitting about a building devoted to glass art being built almost entirely of clear glass. It is also fitting that a glass glass-museum exists in Toledo, Ohio, known as the "Glass City" and home to Libbey Glass since 1888 (Corning, New York, with its eponymous glassmaker could make an equal claim, though its latest expansion, designed by Thomas Phifer and completed in 2015, features solid walls and light-filtering skylights). Libbey's collection of glass art became the foundation of the Toledo Museum of Art's (TMA) world-renowned collection, which eventually led the museum to build a stand-alone building across the street from its Neoclassical 1912 home.

Rather than hold a design competition, as is the norm for museum commissions in the twenty-first century, the TMA hired Japanese architects Kazuyo Sejima (1956–) and Ryue Nishizawa (1966–). Both in their separate practices and together as SANAA, Sejima and Nishizawa are known for amazing effects of transparency and translucency through the use of glass, plastic, and metals in unexpected ways. But when TMA hired SANAA in 2000 the duo had yet to firmly establish that reputation; the Glass Pavilion would become their first completed project in the United States.

The plan of the 76,000 square-foot (7,060 sq. m) single-story building (with full basement) is a simple rectangle with rounded corners. Free of any vertical framing, the 13-foot-high (4 m) laminated glass panes at the perimeter appear to magically support the 2-foot-high (60 cm) solid roof band above it. Thirty-five columns actually do that work, but most of them are hidden in the few rooms (a couple of galleries and service spaces) that are solid rather than glass. The plan is organized as a circuit of bubble-shaped rooms—like a bubble diagram solidified in glass—with galleries, glass "hotshops," multipurpose functions, a café, restrooms, and two courtyards. Between all of the glass surfaces is an inaccessible zone where radiant heating and cooling panels can be found. These services combine with the two layers of glass to create a building-size IGU (insulated glass unit) that provides thermal and acoustic barriers between the different rooms and between the building and its parklike setting.

The technical execution of the all-glass building is remarkable, but the effects are even more so. Reflections, refractions, and overlapping images of the museum, its collection, its visitors, and the surrounding landscape combine into unexpected vistas that make the clear glass a tangible entity, just like the prized objects contained within.

2007 BLOCH BUILDING, NELSON-ATKINS MUSEUM OF ART

Steven Holl Architects ▸ Kansas City, Missouri, United States

Interior view of the lobby lens. The largest of the five lenses includes the lobby, museum store, café, offices, multipurpose rooms, and library, the last to the left of the exposed steel structure.

The Bloch Building seen from the south. The addition's five lenses, made from a cast channel glass that Holl has used on numerous buildings, glow at night from special lighting integrated into the facades.

Any 165,000 square-foot (15,300 sq. m) building is bound to make a statement through size alone. But in the post-Bilbao age when form equals flourish, New York architect Steven Holl (1947–) took a different approach and broke down the scale of his large addition to the Nelson-Atkins Museum of Art by merging landscape and architecture and burying the galleries underground.

Although Holl and his five fellow finalists in a 1999 competition were encouraged to place the expansion to the north of the museum's classically symmetrical 1933 limestone building, Holl sited the building to the east. This tactic preserves views of the old building's north elevation and redefines one edge of the museum's beloved Donald J. Hall Sculpture Park, which gently cascades downhill on the south side of the museum. Holl's design of the Bloch Building is really one huge, 840-foot-long (256 m) building that follows the same descending grade change.

Most notably, the addition pops above the lawn in the form of five glass boxes, what the architect calls "lenses." Glowing in the evening from integral lighting designed by Renfro Design Group, during the day these translucent lenses bring natural light to the below-grade galleries, where the design's flourishes are really found.

With free admission since opening day on June 9, 2007, visitors can enter the Bloch Building at numerous spots: from the sculpture park, from the 1933 building, from the plaza on the north, or from the 500-car parking garage. The last is a treat, since the garage's undulating concrete ceiling is capped by shimmering skylights set into the pool above as part of Walter De Maria's installation *One Sun / 34 Moons*. It's obvious that Holl was considering that people in Kansas City, like most American cities, drive, so the path from the garage is the most thrilling way in, with the northernmost lens (the largest of the five and the only one running north-south rather than east-west) gradually opening up to three stories in height as one ascends the ramp toward the galleries. In this entry hall—scaled for weddings and other events that all museums depend on for revenue—the walls, ramps, stairs, and exposed steel are angular, but curves accompany the angles in the galleries. Here one does not sense the lenses as objects, but only as soft light cascading down the curved ceilings. The formal interplay of the cast-glass lenses, the curved ceilings, and the walls that define a sinuous back-and-forth route in the expansion is mind-boggling at times, but these elements combine to create a peaceful environment where the art can be appreciated free of distraction.

2008 FUNDAÇÃO IBERÊ CAMARGO

Álvaro Siza ▸ **Porto Alegre, Brazil**

Inside the museum's atrium. Visitors are drawn to the small window that looks onto the wide Guaíba River.

The museum seen from the northeast. The building backs up against the cliff walls of an old stone quarry, with its "arms" oriented toward the road and water beyond.

Three "arms" extending from a white, rocklike mass form an immediately memorable image for the museum devoted to the huge collection of Brazilian painter Iberê Camargo. An initial impression of the museum—the first building designed by Portuguese architect Álvaro Siza (1933–) for Brazil—is "architecture as statement," a readymade post-Bilbao icon that is striking yet a bit of a departure from Siza's typically quiet buildings. Yet what looks like an icon for icon's sake is in this case a thoughtful response to the place, the program, and the Expressionist painter's work.

Inaugurated on May 30, 2008, the museum is sited on a former stone quarry immediately adjacent to the four-lane Padre Cacique Avenue alongside the extremely wide Guaíba River. Hired in 2000, Siza realized the narrow site was too small for a program that included galleries for permanent and temporary exhibitions, workshops, an auditorium, a library, a bookstore, a café, offices, storage, and parking. He began by placing the parking in a long rectangle directly beneath the avenue, which freed up the narrow, tapered lot to the south for the rest of the program. The narrow eastern end of the site consists of two volumes that pop up from the basement level and house workshops and a café, the latter adjacent to the small plaza by the museum entrance. The museum sits at the wider western end of the site, rising four stories above plaza level. Its outstretched "arms" create an outdoor void that hints at the indoor atrium behind the undulating wall of white concrete.

The most obvious precedent for the full-height atrium is Frank Lloyd Wright's Solomon R. Guggenheim Museum (see 1959), but whereas Wright's spiral invites an elevator ride to the top and a clockwise descent through the galleries, Siza's system of ramps—along the undulating wall of the atrium and cantilevered outside the building—allows three separate loops for tackling the museum and experiencing Camargo's artworks. The galleries proper form an "L" along the south and west sides of the atrium, corresponding to the flat exterior walls that face the cliffs of the old quarry. Although the galleries can be closed off from each other with 13-foot-tall (4 m) movable walls, the compact plan means that most galleries overlook the atrium, a space that also serves to orient visitors.

Another difference between Wright's and Siza's museums concerns their contexts. Wright closed off his building from the city, as he tended to do, even though Central Park sits right across the street. Siza, on the other hand, provided a few small windows along the ramps that frame the Guaíba River, reminding museumgoers about the artful nature flowing just outside the museum.

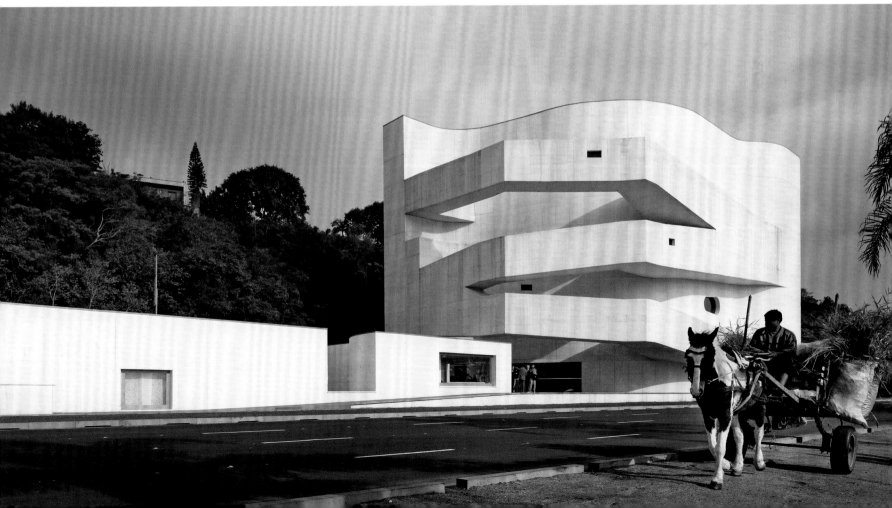

2009 AQUA TOWER

Studio Gang Architects ▸ Chicago, Illinois, United States

Looking up at the tower from the southwest. Gang refers to the portions of the enclosure without balconies as "pools," where high-performance glass is introduced.

Chicago is often considered the birthplace of the skyscraper, due to the steel-frame, curtain wall buildings that began rising in the city during the mid-1880s, yet in the century-plus since the heyday of the so-called Chicago School, the city has seen its share of good and bad skyscraper design—the former highlights mostly in the period between 1950 to 1970, the latter lowlights concentrated after the 1970s. Within this context of a deep tradition of influential tall buildings and a recent past marked by a lack of creativity in considering them artistically, Jeanne Gang's (1964–) Aqua Tower is a breath of fresh air that resonates well beyond the confines of the Windy City.

Aqua Tower is part of Lakeshore East, a primarily residential development east of the Loop and north of Millennium Park that is built on land formerly occupied by a train yard. The 82-story, mixed-use tower is located on the development's western edge, and it consists of rental and condominium residences above a hotel; while Aqua Tower was completed in 2009, the hotel did not open until 2011. The latter's ballrooms, meeting rooms, and other functions are spread out across a large podium that also includes retail, parking, and roof gardens. Nine three-story town houses face the park at the center of the development, and they serve to shield the parking and make a transition from the park at grade to the street raised above the old railroad infrastructure.

Some of the Lakeshore East buildings predating Aqua were uninspiring creations designed by the architecture firm of James Loewenberg, also a head of Magellan Development Group. He hired Gang to give the development a "wow factor," and she delivered with a design where undulating balconies—different on every floor—wrap all four sides of the tower, an otherwise simple box with floor-to-ceiling window walls. The architect justified the balconies as a means of giving residents distant views of Chicago landmarks around nearby buildings, providing opportunities for interaction among other residents, and shading the apartments from the summer sun.

Yet even with these considerations, it's the views looking up at the tower from places like the adjacent park that draw the most attention. Gang likens it to an inhabitable cliff, but the tower's image invites numerous readings, such as sand dunes and waves, none of them right or wrong. Memorable image aside, the undulating balconies in concert with the picket railings serve to eliminate the bird strikes that are all too common with all-glass buildings. Gang's consideration on the behalf of our fine-feathered friends makes the building a good precedent for creatively addressing the issue of bird strikes through design.

2010 MAXXI

Zaha Hadid Architects ▸ Rome, Italy

In the three-story atrium.
Below the skylights are
deep beams that run parallel
to the concrete walls to lead
one's eye and body through
the spaces for art.

MAXXI seen from the east.
The undulating concrete
building forms a plaza in
the northeast corner of the
site, where windows give
glimpses into the galleries,
what Hadid called "suites."

Zaha Hadid (1950–2016) had shown a tendency to design buildings with long, narrow spaces—from the Peak (1982), her competition-winning, unbuilt project for a hillside in Hong Kong, to the Vitra Fire Station (see 1993), her first major built work, to the recent National Museum of XXI Century Arts (MAXXI). In the early days these spaces were within angular buildings, but this century, aided by her associate Patrik Schumacher, they are part of fluid, flowing compositions. MAXXI is a pivotal building in this evolution.

The first phase of the two-phase competition began in 1998, just five years after the completion of the fire station. Early sketches and study models depict the angular forms Hadid still favored then, but by the time they beat out fourteen other finalists two years later, the design had evolved to three undulating, overlapping floors flowing across the L-shaped site.

Located in Rome's outlying Flaminio district, the project involved the demolition of some old military barracks, though the architects retained one and integrated the building into the museum's site. Construction of the primarily poured-in-place concrete building took six years, wrapping up in 2009, when it had a "soft" opening. The building officially opened to the public in 2010.

The three floors of ribbonlike galleries—what the architects call "suites"—unfurl across the site to create a plaza in the northeast corner. Suite V at the top floor projects toward the plaza, a hint at what's happening inside, while the entrance is tucked underneath Suite III, which is propped upon columns more orderly than those at Vitra. The lobby is where the building reveals itself in its wonderful flowing complexity: the three floors converge in a full-height atrium traversed by walkways and stairs. These paths lead to the suites, their linearity accentuated by the parallel trusses supporting the skylights and, occasionally, artworks on display.

With its curling suites, Hadid and Schumacher's MAXXI (it is as much theirs as hers, given his advocacy of parametricism toward the creation of fluid spaces) is like a contemporary update of Frank Lloyd Wright's Guggenheim (see 1959). After all, what are Wright's galleries but long, narrow spaces coiled about an atrium? At MAXXI, a contemporary version of the coil is cut up and unfurled across its three floors, as much a response to its site in Rome as to the art on display.

2011 METROPOL PARASOL

J. Mayer H. ▸ Seville, Spain

The Setas de la Encarnación seen from the south. The huge structure lifted on six large columns recalls utopian visions of floating or elevated cities from the 1970s.

Look at a map of Seville's Casco Antiguo and directly in the center of the roughly oval area is the Plaza de la Encarnación, now home to what is popularly known as Setas de la Encarnación (Encarnación's mushrooms). When plans for an expansion of the car park previously on the site unearthed Roman archaeological ruins, Seville launched an international competition in 2004 asking entrants to envision ideas for the square that would respect the newly discovered past, provide some commercial activity, and give the city an icon to draw tourists, like Gehry's addition to Bilbao did in 1997. German architect Jürgen Mayer H. (1965–) won with his Metropol Parasol entry.

Designed to provide shade to the large 230 × 490 foot (70 × 150 m) plaza, the Metropol Parasol, lifted 90 feet (28 m) in the air on six large columns, is a lattice made from laminated wood and steel joined at over 3,000 connection points by heat-resistant glue. Like Frank Gehry's Guggenheim Museum Bilbao, the parasol is a complex construction that could only have been realized with computer modeling. Each piece of laminated wood is uniquely shaped, a fact that can be grasped from below as well as above, via the walkway that offers visitors panoramic views of the city's rooftops.

The rooftop walkway and observatory is the uppermost of four vertical striations. Lowest is the museum devoted to the archaeological ruins, and above it, at the grade of the surrounding streets, are the commercial spaces—part mall, part market. These lower levels were designed by other architects, so they do not carry the same iconic expression as Jürgen Mayer H.'s creation overhead, which begins at the plaza level—the third of the four levels—sitting above the shops. Reached by stairs from the north or south, or from elevators in the most central of the six hollow columns, the plaza is used for concerts and other events, or just as a place to get some shade in sunny Seville.

A lot changed in Spain in the seven years between the competition win and the structure's inauguration on March 27, 2011. Any optimism that existed in 2004 dissolved over time as the construction lagged, the budget increased, and the country spiraled into a recession more damaging than in most European countries. Critics lambasted the excess and the extra millions needed to complete it, but some optimism returned with the completion of the exuberant parasol/mushrooms, a futuristic jolt in the city's medieval core.

2012 CCTV HEADQUARTERS

Office for Metropolitan Architecture ▸ Beijing, China

Aerial view from the southwest. Although only 52 stories at its highest point, the coiled skyscraper contains more than 5 million square feet (473,000 sq. m), the same as one of the 110-story Twin Towers destroyed on September 11, 2001.

"Go East" was the mantra that Rem Koolhaas (1944–) and his compatriots at the Office for Metropolitan Architecture (OMA) spouted at the turn of the century, most notably in response to questions about their omission from the World Trade Center rebuilding process in 2002. With a sense of duty to participate in at least one project in rapidly urbanizing China, that same year OMA received the most high-profile commission in the country: the headquarters for China Central Television (CCTV) in Beijing's new Central Business District. Initially set for completion in time for the 2008 Summer Olympics, the project did not have its official completion ceremony until May 2012.

Frustrated with the default condition of the extruded skyscraper and the race to build taller, Koolhaas, Ole Scheeren, David Gianotten, and the rest of the OMA team proposed a closed loop for CCTV's television studios, offices, broadcasting, and production facilities: two leaning towers rise from an L-shaped base and come together in a 250 foot (75 m) cantilevered overhang 37 stories above the street. This tactic was founded on the desire to foster interconnectivity between departments, but with production facilities in the base, research facilities and offices in the towers, and executives in the overhang, the building reinforces the corporate hierarchy of traditional skyscrapers—or even a nontraditional one like the Ford Foundation (see 1968). As a form, the building is an expression of the process of TV production, but within the city it is purely an icon, distinct from everything around it, especially with its appearance constantly changing depending on one's position. (A more sedate companion to CCTV Headquarters sits across the street: the Television Cultural Center [TVCC], also designed by Koolhaas, completed in 2010, one year after it was damaged in a fire caused by fireworks.)

With such a bold reconsideration of the skyscraper—a thickened Möbius strip up to 52 stories tall—structural engineering was as important as architectural expression. Koolhaas worked with longtime collaborator Cecil Balmond, who designed the structure such that the concrete cores take most of the gravity loads, while a diamond steel mesh applied to the exterior glass walls braces the building from lateral forces. Instead of a consistent pattern across the facades, the mesh is irregular—dense and closed in some places, open and broken in others—to express the forces working on the building. These lines are layered over the activities inside, which include public access via a dedicated loop that leads to an observation deck at the top of the overhang. From here there are expansive views of Beijing through the glass walls, as well as vertiginous views of the ground below through circular glass floors.

2013 XIANGSHAN CAMPUS, CHINA ACADEMY OF ART

Amateur Architecture Studio ▸ Hangzhou, China

View of the Guesthouse from the south. A series of six parallel buildings are united by a sawtooth roof and a palette of brick, wood, and rammed earth.

View of the second phase. With millions of salvaged roof tiles reused throughout the campus, the roof is the bastion of tradition, here recalling Chinese calligraphy.

When Chinese architect Wang Shu (1963–) was named the 2012 laureate of the Pritzker Architecture Prize, the collective question around the world was "Who?" Then, as journalists reported on his notable buildings, especially the Ningbo History Museum (2008), the attention shifted to the omission of his wife and professional partner, Lu Wenyu (as of 2015 only two women have won the Pritzker Prize: Zaha Hadid and Kazuyo Sejima, the latter with SANAA partner Ryue Nishizawa). Yet to hear Wang Shu speak about his architecture is to hear him speak about *their* architecture, a collective product with a strong focus on merging the traditional with the contemporary. The collaborative approach and appreciation of the vernacular is evident in the name of their firm: Amateur Architecture Studio.

While the museum in Ningbo has become their best-known project since 2012, the Xiangshan Campus for the China Academy of Art (CAA) is their largest, composed of over thirty buildings with an area of 5.4 million square feet (500,000 sq. m) executed in multiple phases and built around a hill and two streams in Hangzhou's Zhuantang Town. The first phase was completed in 2004 to the north of the hill with nearly a dozen buildings modeled as free interpretations of traditional Chinese courtyard buildings. Links to the past were strengthened through the reuse of millions of tiles from houses demolished in the Zhejiang province for the new buildings' roofs. The second phase, completed in 2007, extended the campus south of the hill with fifteen unique buildings based on four novel types, such as "combined courtyard" and "huge hill house." Details like the recycled tile roofs continued, even as the forms were freer than in the first phase; continuity between the two phases was nevertheless evident.

The third phase, the Guesthouse, was completed in 2013 on a long and narrow stream-front site between the hill and the second phase. The design began similarly to the second phase, with linked courtyards, but departed thanks to a longer design period than the previous phases. A large serrated roof, covered with the usual tiles, shelters a series of rammed-earth dwellings perpendicular to the water. The artistic treatment of the roof structure and the openings in some end walls reinforces the difference between this latest phase and the previous two, while perhaps signaling the direction for any future buildings.

As the chair of the Department of Art & Architecture at the CAA, Wang Shu is as much client as architect, yet he does not have a monopoly on campus buildings, as the CAA realized a folk art museum designed by Kengo Kuma rather than its favorite architect—and his wife.

2014 MARKTHAL

MVRDV ▸ Rotterdam, Netherlands

Markthal seen from the east. The super-clear glass that caps each end of the market allows views through the building, but it also displays the colorful mural with larger-than-life fruits, vegetables, plants, and even insects.

In the 1972 book *Learning from Las Vegas*, Robert Venturi, Denise Scott Brown, and Steven Izenour famously defined the Decorated Shed as a boxy, loftlike building that used signage to communicate its function; the Las Vegas strip was the most concentrated example of this American vernacular. The authors positioned the Decorated Shed in opposition to Ducks—so-named for Long Island's "The Big Duck" that looks exactly like it sounds—buildings that used form to communicate function. Regardless of one's preference—be it for Modern Ducks or postmodern Sheds—the book managed to influence architectural discourse so much that all subsequent buildings fit into either camp. But some buildings bridge these two realms, such as Markthal (Market Hall) in Rotterdam, a surreal combination of 228 apartments and a 100-stall market opened by Queen Maxima in October 2014.

The need for the Markthal in central Rotterdam arose from a new law in the Netherlands that required once open-air meat and fish stalls to move indoors for reasons of hygiene. The Dutch firm MVRDV (founded in 1993 by Winy Maas, Jacob van Rijs, and Nathalie de Vries) teamed up with developer Provast and won an invited competition in 2004 with their proposal to combine the market hall and housing into one building. The apartments—a mix of rental and market-rate units—are placed in an arching structure next to and over the vaulted market hall. Terraces give the apartments views of the Grote of Sint-Laurenskerk and other parts of the surrounding city, while sound- and smell-proof windows give the residents views into the market hall; the penthouse units actually have glass floors that look into the space! Within the Duck/Shed dichotomy set up by Venturi, Scott Brown, and Izenour, the apartments give the building a Duck-like presence.

The Decorated Shed occurs inside the market hall, specifically *Cornucopia*, the digitally printed mural by artists Arno Coenen and Iris Roskam that covers the 118,000 square-foot (11,000 sq. m) surface of the vaulted interior. Oversize images of fruits and vegetables act as signage for the market, aided by the highly transparent glass hung in cable-net facades at both ends of the 400-foot-long (120 m) space. In addition to the market and housing, the mixed-use building includes retail, restaurants, underground parking, and a supermarket, all meant to give the building vitality even when the market is closed. But the focus, as the giant snap peas overhead attest, is the market. All the better reason to visit and eat at one of the stalls with a rooftop terrace under the colors and windows of a unique hybrid.

2015 THE BROAD

Diller Scofidio + Renfro ▸ Los Angeles, California, United States

Third-floor gallery. The galleries upstairs sit directly on top of the Vault in a column-free space that is 200 feet (61 m) square and illuminated by skylights angled to the north.

Grand Avenue elevation on the south. The glow of the galleries atop the building above the darkness of the Vault can be sensed through the spongelike Veil.

It seems fitting to wrap up *100 Buildings, 100 Years* by comparing and contrasting the first building, H. P. Berlage's Holland House (see 1916), with this last building designed by Diller Scofidio + Renfro (DS+R: Elizabeth Diller, Ricardo Scofidio, and Charles Renfro). Holland House is an office building; the Broad is an art museum. Holland House was designed for a Dutch shipping company; the Broad was designed for Eli and Edythe L. Broad, billionaire philanthropists and art collectors. Holland House was designed by an Amsterdam architect for a site in London; the Broad was designed by a New York firm for a site in Los Angeles. The facades of Holland House look solid from an oblique angle; those of the Broad look solid from just about any angle. Even though the buildings are different functionally and geographically, this last trait, though hardly unique to both buildings, is a telling one: as styles and technologies change, the facade continues to be the most important means of architectural expression, particularly in urban areas.

"The Veil" is the name given to the facade that wraps all four sides of the Broad. Its two main faces are on Grand Avenue to the east, and toward Frank Gehry's Walt Disney Concert Hall (2003) to the north. Made up of 2,500 glass fiber reinforced concrete (GFRC) panels in nearly 400 unique shapes, the Veil conceals and reveals the three floors of the museum: the lobby on the ground floor, the "Vault" in the middle, and the gallery below a grid of veil-like skylights on the top floor. The Vault is the most unique aspect of the Broad, since it serves as storage for Eli and Edythe Broad's extensive collection that they loan out to institutions. Its inclusion makes the building as much warehouse as museum. DS+R treated the vault like a solid mass pierced by the elevator, escalator, and stair, the last offering glimpses into the art storage through windows at intermediate landings.

The facade gives little indication as to what sits behind it, excepting in a few places: the Veil is "lifted" at the corners on Grand to provide visual and physical access to the lobby, and it is indented at the "Oculus"—like a thumb mushed into a sponge—in the middle of the same elevation to signal the lecture hall on the second floor. Unlike the grid of vertical piers and horizontal windows and spandrels at Holland House (and numerous other twentieth-century buildings), the angled GFRC panels belie the contents, which are solid (storage) and transparent (galleries) but treated uniformly. A product of twenty-first-century digital design and fabrication, the facade looks repetitive but is highly variable—a bespoke cover for a bespoke art collection.

TIMELINE

1916 Holland House | Hendrik Petrus Berlage | London, England

Woodbury County Courthouse | William L. Steele | Sioux City, Iowa, United States

▸ New York establishes the first US zoning law.

1917 Crypt of the Colònia Güell | Antoni Gaudí | Barcelona, Spain

El Molino | Francisco Gianotti | Buenos Aires, Argentina

▸ D'Arcy Wentworth Thompson's *On Growth and Form* published.
▸ De Stijl movement founded in Amsterdam.
▸ Tony Garnier's *Cité Industrielle* published.

1918 Hallidie Building | Willis Polk | San Francisco, California, United States

Park Meerwijk | J. F. Staal et al. | Bergen, Netherlands

▸ J. J. P. Oud's essay "Architecture and Standardization in Mass Construction" published.

1919 Helsinki Central Railway Station | Eliel Saarinen | Helsinki, Finland

▸ Bruno Taut's *Alpine Architecture* published.
▸ Walter Gropius founds Bauhaus in Weimar, Germany.

1920 Het Schip | Michel de Klerk | Amsterdam, Netherlands

▸ Charles-Édouard Jeanneret-Gris adopts the pseudonym Le Corbusier.
▸ Vladimir Tatlin designs Monument to the Third International, also known as Tatlin's Tower.

1921 Einsteinturm | Erich Mendelsohn | Potsdam, Germany

Hollyhock House | Frank Lloyd Wright | Los Angeles, California, United States

▸ Ludwig Mies van der Rohe unveils his design of the Friedrichstrasse Office Building.

1922 Schindler House | Rudolph M. Schindler | Los Angeles, California, United States

▸ Competition held for the Chicago Tribune Tower.

1923 Notre Dame du Raincy | Auguste Perret | Raincy, France

Chilehaus | Fritz Höger | Hamburg, Germany

Fiat Factory | Giacomo Mattè-Trucco | Turin, Italy

Imperial Hotel | Frank Lloyd Wright | Inuyama, Japan

Stockholm City Hall | Ragnar Östberg | Stockholm, Sweden

▸ Le Corbusier's *Vers une architecture* published.
▸ Auguste Perret founds *L'Architecture Vivante* magazine.

▸ Frank Lloyd Wright's Imperial Hotel survives the Great Japan Earthquake.

1924 Rietveld Schröder House | Gerrit Rietveld | Utrecht, Netherlands

Police Headquarters | Hack Kampmann | Copenhagen, Denmark

▸ Ludwig Hilberseimer designs his Hochhausstadt (High-rise City) project.

1925 Pavillon de l'Esprit Nouveau | Le Corbusier | Bologna, Italy

First Church of Christ the Scientist | Hendrik Petrus Berlage | The Hague, Netherlands

Maisons La Roche-Jeanneret | Le Corbusier | Paris, France

▸ International Exposition of Modern Industrial and Decorative Arts held in Paris.

1926 Bauhaus Dessau | Walter Gropius | Dessau, Germany

▸ Gruppo 7 formed by Giuseppe Terragni and others in Italy.
▸ Competition held for the League of Nations.
▸ Le Corbusier issues his "Five Points of a New Architecture."
▸ Sunnyside Gardens completed in Queens, New York.

1927 Grundtvigs Kirke | Peder Vilhelm Jensen-Klint | Copenhagen, Denmark

Rue Mallet-Stevens Houses | Robert Mallet-Stevens | Paris, France

St. Antonius Church | Karl Moser | Basel, Switzerland

▸ Deutscher Werkbund exhibition, including the Weissenhof Estate, held in Stuttgart, Germany.

1928 Goetheanum | Rudolf Steiner | Dornach, Switzerland

Petersdorff Department Store | Erich Mendelsohn | Wroclaw, Poland

Rusakov Workers' Club | Konstantin Melnikov | Moscow, Russia

Stockholm Public Library | Gunnar Asplund | Stockholm, Sweden

Zonnestraal Sanatorium | Bijvoet & Duiker | Hilversum, Netherlands

▸ Congrès International d'Architecture Moderne (CIAM) founded.
▸ Competition held for the Columbus Memorial Lighthouse in the Dominican Republic.
▸ Giò Ponti founds *Domus* magazine.

1929 Barcelona Pavilion | Ludwig Mies van der Rohe | Barcelona, Spain

E1027 | Eileen Gray | Roquebrune-Cap-Martin, France

Melnikov House | Konstantin Melnikov | Moscow, Russia

Novocomum | Giuseppe Terragni | Como, Italy

Saarinen House | Eliel Saarinen | Bloomfield Hills, Michigan, United States

Universum Cinema | Erich Mendelsohn | Berlin, Germany

▶ Frank Lloyd Wright's Midway Gardens demolished in Chicago.
▶ Le Corbusier's *The City of To-morrow and Its Planning* published.
▶ Le Corbusier first travels to Latin America.
▶ Radburn, "a town for the motor age," founded in New Jersey.
▶ Union des Artistes Moderne (UAM) founded in France.

1930 Villa Tugendhat | Ludwig Mies van der Rohe | Brno, Czech Republic

Chrysler Building | William Van Alen | New York City, United States

Garrison Church of St. Martin | Arthur Gordon Shoosmith New Dehli, India

Van Nelle Factory | Brinkman & Van der Vlugt, Mart Stam | Rotterdam, Netherlands

Villa Müller | Adolf Loos | Prague, Czech Republic

▶ Adolf Loos develops the Raumplan.
▶ Insulated glass made commercially available.

1931 Villa Savoye | Le Corbusier | Poissy, France

Christ the King Church | Barry Byrne | Cork, Ireland

Empire State Building | Shreve, Lamb & Harmon | New York City, United States

Hilversum Town Hall | Willem Dudok | Hilversum, Netherlands

▶ Empire State Building becomes the world's tallest building.
▶ Competition held for the Palace of the Soviets.
▶ Window air conditioner invented.

1932 PSFS Building | Howe and Lescaze | Philadelphia, Pennsylvania, United States

Church of the Most Sacred Heart of Our Lord | Jože Plečnik | Prague, Czech Republic

House and Studio of Diego Rivera and Frida Kahlo | Juan O'Gorman | Mexico City, Mexico

Neutra VDL Studio and Residences | Richard Neutra | Los Angeles, California, United States

▶ Frank Lloyd Wright forms the Taliesin Fellowship.

▶ The Museum of Modern Art, New York (MoMA) holds its *International Exhibition of Modern Architecture*.
▶ LEGO founded in Denmark.
▶ Sydney Harbour Bridge opens in Australia.

1933 Haus Schminke | Hans Scharoun | Löbau, Germany

Paimio Sanitorium | Alvar Aalto | Paimio, Finland

Quartier des Etats-Unis Housing Development | Tony Garnier | Lyon, France

▶ Century of Progress International Exhibition held in Chicago.
▶ CIAM's *Charter of Athens* published.
▶ Iakov Chernikov self-publishes *Architectural Fantasies: 101 Compositions*.
▶ Nazi government closes Bauhaus in Dessau, Germany.

1934 Isokon, Lawn Road Flats | Wells Coates | London, England

Penguin Pool | Berthold Lubetkin | London, England

▶ National Socialist Party of Germany bans the Deutscher Werkbund.
▶ Frank Lloyd Wright unveils his Broadacre City model in New York.

1935 De La Warr Pavilion | Erich Mendelsohn and Serge Chermayeff | Bexhill-on-Sea, England

Municipal Museum | Hendrik Petrus Berlage | The Hague, Netherlands

Prague Castle Remodeling | Jože Plečnik | Prague, Czech Republic

Santa Maria Novella Railway Station | Gruppo Toscano | Florence, Italy

Vyborg Library | Alvar Aalto | Vyborg, Russia

▶ Alvar Aalto et al. forms Artek in Finland.
▶ Works Progress Administration (WPA) forms in the United States.
▶ Le Corbusier's *La Ville Radieuse* published.

1936 Casa del Fascio | Giuseppe Terragni | Como, Italy

Max Liebling House | Dov Karmi | Tel Aviv, Israel

Schocken House Offices and Library | Erich Mendelsohn | Jerusalem, Israel

▶ Le Corbusier makes a second trip to Latin America.

1937 Taliesin West | Frank Lloyd Wright | Scottsdale, Arizona, United States

Central Market | Jean Desbois, Louis Chauchon | Phnom Penh, Cambodia

Sant'Elia Nursery School | Giuseppe Terragni | Como, Italy

▶ Golden Gate Bridge completed in San Francisco.
▶ Walter Gropius teaches at Harvard University.

1938 **Fallingwater | Frank Lloyd Wright | Mill Run, Pennsylvania, United States**

Gropius House | Walter Gropius | Lincoln, Massachusetts, United States

Kröller-Müller Museum | Henry van de Velde | Otterlo, Netherlands

Moscow Metro | Metrostroy | Moscow, Russia

Museum of Modern Art | Philip Goodwin and Edward Durell Stone | New York City, United States

▸ Frank Lloyd Wright appears on the cover of *Time* magazine.

1939 **Villa Mairea | Alvar Aalto | Noormarkku, Finland**

▸ European diaspora disperses architects to the Americas.
▸ MoMA opens on Fifty-Third Street in Midtown Manhattan.
▸ New York World's Fair held.

1940 **Skogskyrkogården | Gunnar Asplund and Sigurd Lewerentz | Enskede, Sweden**

Rockefeller Center | Raymond Hood | New York City, United States

Workers' Association | Ove Bang | Oslo, Norway

▸ Armour Institute and Lewis Institute merge to form Illinois Institute of Technology (IIT) in Chicago.

1941 **National and University Library | Jože Plečnik | Ljubljana, Slovenia**

Red Rocks Amphitheater | Burnham Hoyt | Morrison, Colorado, United States

Resurrection Chapel | Erik Bryggman | Turku, Finland

▸ Sigfried Giedion's *Space, Time and Architecture* published.

1942 **Cranbrook Academy of Art | Eliel Saarinen | Bloomfield Hills, Michigan, United States**

Arthur Neiva Pavilion | Jorge Ferreira | Rio de Janeiro, Brazil

First Christian Church | Eliel Saarinen | Columbus, Indiana, United States

Palazzo della Civiltà Italiana Monument | Giovanni Guerrini et al. | Rome, Italy

▸ Casa Malaparte completed in Capri, Italy.
▸ Esposizione Universale planned for Rome but canceled due to World War II.

1943 **Ministry of Education and Health | Le Corbusier and Lúcio Costa | Rio de Janeiro, Brazil**

Université de Montréal | Ernest Cormier | Montreal, Canada

▸ Ayn Rand's *The Fountainhead* published.
▸ MoMA holds *Brazil Builds* exhibition.

1944 **Solimar Building | Manuel Copado | Havana, Cuba**

▸ Jean Prouvé designs the Demountable House.

1945 **Casa del Puente | Amancio Williams | Mar del Plata, Argentina**

Golconde Dormitory | Antonin Raymond | Puducherry, India

▸ Architect Albert Speer tried at Nuremberg Trials and sentenced to twenty years in prison.
▸ Bombing of Dresden.
▸ John Entenza starts the Case Study House Program.

1946 **Dymaxion Dwelling Machine | R. Buckminster Fuller | Dearborn, Michigan, United States**

▸ William Zeckendorf proposes an airport the size of Central Park on Manhattan's West Side.

1947 **Pampulha | Oscar Niemeyer | Belo Horizonte, Brazil**

New Gourna Village | Hassan Fathy | Luxor, Egypt

▸ Eleven architects, including Le Corbusier and Oscar Niemeyer, team up to design the United Nations Headquarters in New York.
▸ R. Buckminster Fuller invents the Geodesic Dome.

1948 **Casa Luis Barragán | Luis Barragán | Mexico City, Mexico**

Baker House | Alvar Aalto | Cambridge, Massachusetts, United States

Equitable Savings and Loan Association Headquarters | Pietro Belluschi | Portland, Oregon, United States

▸ International Union of Architects (UIA) forms in Switzerland.
▸ Moscow allows the construction of "tall buildings."

1949 **Glass House | Philip Johnson | New Canaan, Connecticut, United Staes**

Eames House | Charles & Ray Eames | Pacific Palisades, California, United States

V. C. Morris Gift Shop | Frank Lloyd Wright | San Francisco, California, United States

▸ Housing Act passes in the United States.

1950 **Johnson Wax Buildings | Frank Lloyd Wright | Racine, Wisconsin, United States**

Christ Church Lutheran | Eliel Saarinen | Minneapolis, Minnesota, United States

National Theatre of Iceland | Guðjón Samúelsson | Reykjavík, Iceland

Oslo City Hall | Arnstein Arneberg, Magnus Poulsson | Oslo, Norway

Turin Exhibition Hall | Pier Luigi Nervi | Turin, Italy

- Le Corbusier's *Le Modulor* published.
- Bruno Zevi's *Towards an Organic Architecture* published.
- Frank Lloyd Wright's Larkin Building (1904) in Buffalo demolished.

1951 **Farnsworth House | Ludwig Mies van der Rohe | Plano, Illinois, United States**

860–880 Lake Shore Drive | Ludwig Mies van der Rohe | Chicago, Illinois, United States

Casa Il Girasole | Luigi Moretti | Rome, Italy

- Festival of Britain held.
- First Levittown completed on Long Island, New York.

1952 **Säynätsalo Town Hall | Alvar Aalto | Säynätsalo, Finland**

Housing for Borsalino Employees | Ignazio Gardella | Alessandria, Italy

Lever House | Skidmore, Owings & Merrill | New York City, United States

Unité d'Habitation | Le Corbusier | Marseille, France

1953 **Cuidad Universitaria de Caracas | Carlos Raúl Villanueva Caracas, Venezuela**

United Nations Headquarters | Harrison & Abramovitz | New York City, United States

Universidad Nacional Autónoma de México (UNAM) | Mario Pani et al. | Mexico City, Mexico

- Alcoa Building, first skyscraper with all-aluminum facade, completed in Pittsburgh.
- Museo Experimental El Eco opens in Mexico City.
- Team X forms in opposition to CIAM.

1954 **Mill Owners' Association Building | Le Corbusier | Ahmedabad, India**

ATBAT Collective Housing | Shadrach Woods et al. | Casablanca, Morocco

Casa de la Marina | Josep Coderch | Barcelona, Spain

Solimene Ceramic Factory | Paolo Soleri | Vietri sul Mare, Italy

Yale University Art Gallery | Louis I. Kahn | New Haven, Connecticut, United States

- Martin Heidegger's essay "Building, Dwelling, Thinking" published.
- Victor Gruen's Northland Center, precursor to the shopping mall, opens in Detroit.

1955 **Notre Dame du Haut | Le Corbusier | Ronchamp, France**

Capilla de las Capuchinas Sacramentarias | Luis Barragán | Mexico City, Mexico

Church de la Virgen Milagrosa | Félix Candela | Mexico City, Mexico

MIT Chapel | Eero Saarinen | Cambridge, Massachusetts, United States

Ulm School of Design | Max Bill | Ulm, Germany

- Disneyland opens in Anaheim, California.
- MoMA holds *Latin American Architecture since 1945* exhibition.
- Prudential Building, the first skyscraper in Chicago since 1934, completed.

1956 **S. R. Crown Hall | Ludwig Mies van der Rohe | Chicago, Illinois, United States**

Chapel of the Holy Cross | Anshen and Allen | Sedona, Arizona, United States

Peace Pavilion | Kenzō Tange | Hiroshima, Japan

Price Tower | Frank Lloyd Wright | Bartlesville, Oklahoma, United States

- Eero Saarinen appears on the cover of *Time* magazine.
- Federal Aid Highway Act passes in the United States.
- Victor Gruen's Southdale Center, the first traditional shopping mall, opens in Edina, Minnesota.

1957 **Miller House and Garden | Eero Saarinen | Columbus, Indiana, United States**

Climat de France Housing Complex | Fernand Pouillon | Algiers, Algeria

La Merced Market | Enrique del Moral | Mexico City, Mexico

Otaniemi Chapel | Heikki and Kaija Siren | Espoo, Finland

- Competition held for the Sydney Opera House.

1958 **Seagram Building | Ludwig Mies van der Rohe | New York City, United States**

David S. Ingalls Skating Rink | Eero Saarinen | New Haven, Connecticut, United States

Inland Steel Building | Skidmore, Owings & Merrill | Chicago, Illinois, United States

Los Manantiales Restaurant | Félix Candela | Mexico City, Mexico

Torre Velasca | Lodovico Belgiojoso, Enrico Peressutti, and Ernest Rogers | Milan, Italy

- Brussels World's Fair held.

1959 **Solomon R. Guggenheim Museum | Frank Lloyd Wright | New York City, United States**

Beth Sholom Synagogue | Frank Lloyd Wright | Elkins Park, Pennsylvania, United States

Church of the Three Crosses | Alvar Aalto | Vuoksenniska, Finland

Edifício COPAN | Oscar Niemeyer | São Paulo, Brazil

National Museum of Western Art | Le Corbusier | Tokyo, Japan

- CIAM disbands.

1960 **Church of Christ Obrero | Eladio Dieste | Atlántida, Uruguay**

Couvent Sainte-Marie de la Tourette | Le Corbusier | Éveux-sur-l'Arbresle, France

National Congress | Oscar Niemeyer | Brasília, Brazil

Roofless Church | Philip Johnson | New Harmony, Indiana, United States

St. Mark's Church | Sigurd Lewerentz | Stockholm, Sweden

▶ Brasília inaugurated as Brazil's new capital.

▶ Kevin Lynch's *The Image of the City* published.

▶ *Metabolism 1960 – The Proposals for a New Urbanism* manifesto released in Japan.

▶ R. Buckminster Fuller envisions an energy-saving dome over Midtown Manhattan.

▶ Reyner Banham's *Theory and Design in the First Machine Age* published.

1961 **Saint John's Abbey Church | Marcel Breuer | Collegeville, Minnesota, United States**

Chapel of Futuna | John Scott | Wellington, New Zealand

Dhahran Airport | Minoru Yamasaki | Dhahran, Saudi Arabia

Gandhi Bhawan | Pierre Jeanneret | Chandigarh, India

Gunma Music Center | Antonin Raymond | Takasaki, Japan

▶ Construction of the Berlin Wall begins.

▶ Jane Jacobs's *The Death and Life of Great American Cities* published.

▶ First issue of *Archigram* magazine released.

▶ Le Corbusier appears on the cover of *Time* magazine.

▶ New York City reforms its 1916 zoning law.

1962 **Nordic Pavilion | Sverre Fehn | Venice, Italy**

Anglican Cathedral of the Holy Cross | Hope, Reeler and Morris | Lusaka, Zambia

Marin County Civic Center | Frank Lloyd Wright | San Rafael, California, United States

St. Theresia Church | Rudolf Schwarz | Linz, Austria

TWA Terminal | Eero Saarinen | New York City, United States

▶ Start of Second Vatican Council, which impacts the form of churches.

1963 **Yale Art and Architecture Building | Paul Rudolph | New Haven, Connecticut, United States**

Beinecke Rare Book and Manuscript Library | Skidmore, Owings & Merrill | New Haven, Connecticut, United States

Carpenter Center for the Visual Arts | Le Corbusier | Cambridge, Massachusetts, United States

Leicester University Engineering Building | James Stirling | Leicester, England

Philharmonie | Hans Scharoun | Berlin, Germany

United States Air Force Academy Cadet Chapel | Skidmore, Owings & Merrill | Colorado, United States

▶ Ada Louise Huxtable becomes the first architecture critic at the *New York Times*.

▶ New York's Pennsylvania Station demolished.

▶ Serge Chermayeff and Christopher Alexander's *Community and Privacy* published.

1964 **Yoyogi National Gymnasium | Kenzō Tange | Tokyo, Japan**

Economist Building | Alison and Peter Smithson | London, England

Maeght Foundation | Josep Lluís Sert | Saint-Paul-de-Vence, France

Marina City | Bertrand Goldberg | Chicago, Illinois, United States

Museo di Castelvecchio | Carlo Scarpa | Verona, Italy

San Giovanni Battista Motorway Church | Giovanni Michelucci | Florence, Italy

▶ Archigram designs the Plug-in City.

▶ MoMA exhibits Bernard Rudofsky's *Architecture Without Architects*.

▶ Cedric Price designs his Fun Palace.

▶ R. Buckminster Fuller on the cover of *Time* magazine.

▶ Robert Venturi designs the Vanna Venturi House in Philadelphia.

1965 **Salk Institute | Louis I. Kahn | San Diego, California, United States**

Capitol Complex | Le Corbusier | Chandigarh, India

Northern Aviary | Cedric Price et al. | London, England

Sea Ranch Condominium I | Moore, Lyndon, Turnbull, Whitaker | Sea Ranch, California, United States

Shrine of the Book | Frederick Kiesler | Jerusalem, Israel

▶ Construction of National Art Schools halted in Cuba.

▶ Drop City founded in Colorado.

▶ Eero Saarinen's Gateway Arch completed in St. Louis.

▶ Meiji-mura open-air architecture museum opens in Japan.

1966 **Bank of London and South America | Clorindo Testa and SEPRA | Buenos Aires, Argentina**

CEPAL Building | Emilio Duhart | Santiago, Chile

Kyoto International Conference Center | Sachio Otani | Kyoto, Japan

Saint Petri Church | Sigurd Lewerentz | Klippan, Sweden

Whitney Museum of American Art | Marcel Breuer | New York City, United States

▶ Aldo Rossi's *The Architecture of the City* published.

▶ Robert Venturi's *Complexity and Contradiction in Architecture* published.

▶ U.S. National Historic Preservation Act passes.

1967 **Habitat 67 | Moshe Safdie | Montreal, Canada**

Bensberg Town Hall | Gottfried Böhm | Bensberg, Germany

Shizuoka Press and Broadcasting Center | Kenzō Tange | Tokyo, Japan

▸ Alvar Aalto Medal established.

▸ Expo 67 held in Montreal.

▸ Frank Lloyd Wright's Imperial Hotel demolished.

▸ Jacques Tati's *Playtime* released.

1968 **Ford Foundation | Kevin Roche John Dinkeloo and Associates | New York City, United States**

Cuadra San Cristóbal | Luis Barragán | Mexico City, Mexico

Museu de Arte de São Paulo (MASP) | Lina Bo Bardi | São Paulo, Brazil

Neue Nationalgalerie | Ludwig Mies van der Rohe | Berlin, Germany

St. Mary's Church | Douglas Cardinal | Red Deer, Alberta, Canada

▸ Charles and Ray Eames's *Powers of Ten* released.

▸ Mexico City hosts the Summer Olympics.

1969 **Faculdade de Arquitetura e Urbanismo da Universidade de São Paulo | João Batista Vilanova Artigas and Carlos Cascaldi | São Paulo, Brazil**

Cultural Center of the Philippines | Leandro V. Locsin | Manila, Philippines

Gihindamuyaga Monastery | Lucien Kroll | Butare, Rwanda

Oakland Museum of California | Kevin Roche John Dinkeloo and Associates | Oakland, California, United States

Tuskegee Chapel | Paul Rudolph | Tuskegee, Alabama, United States

▸ Hassan Fathy's *Architecture for the Poor: An Experiment in Rural Egypt* published.

▸ The "New York Five" assembles at MoMA.

▸ Reyner Banham's *Architecture of the Well-tempered Environment* published.

1970 **Catedral de Brasília | Oscar Niemeyer | Brasília, Brazil**

Brunswick Centre | Patrick Hodgkinson | London, England

John Hancock Center | Skidmore, Owings & Merrill | Chicago, Illinois, United States

Standard Bank Centre | HPP | Johannesburg, South Africa

Torres del Parque Apartment Buildings | Rogelio Salmona | Bogotá, Colombia

▸ Ciudad Abierta (Open City) created in Chile.

▸ Construction of Paolo Soleri's Arcosanti begins in Arizona.

▸ Expo '70, the first world's fair in Japan, held in Osaka.

▸ First Earth Day celebration held in the United States.

1971 **Phillips Exeter Academy Library | Louis I. Kahn | Exeter, New Hampshire, United States**

Cathedral of Saint Mary of the Assumption | Pietro Belluschi and Pier Luigi Nervi | San Francisco, California, United States

Denver Art Museum | Giò Ponti | Denver, Colorado, United States

Finlandia Hall | Alvar Aalto | Helsinki, Finland

Iglesia San Pedro | Eladio Dieste | Durazno, Uruguay

▸ *a+u* magazine founded in Japan.

▸ "Freetown" Christiania established on a former military base in Denmark.

▸ Competition held for Paris's Centre Georges Pompidou.

▸ Disney World opens in Orlando, Florida.

1972 **Kimbell Art Museum | Louis I. Kahn | Fort Worth, Texas, United States**

Munich Olympic Stadium | Günther Behnisch and Frei Otto | Munich, Germany

Nakagin Capsule Tower | Kisho Kurokawa | Tokyo, Japan

Permanent Exhibition Complex | Raj Rewal | New Dehli, India

▸ Pruitt-Igoe, a public housing project designed by Minoru Yamasaki in St. Louis, demolished.

▸ Robert Venturi, Denise Scott Brown, and Steven Izenour's *Learning from Las Vegas* published.

▸ Munich hosts the Summer Olympics.

▸ UNESCO adopts the World Heritage preservation treaty.

1973 **Sydney Opera House | Jørn Utzon | Sydney, Australia**

Federal Reserve Bank of Minneapolis | Gunnar Birkerts | Minneapolis, Minnesota, United States

Hyatt Regency Hotel | John Portman | San Francisco, California, United States

Kenyatta International Conference Centre | Karl Henrik Nøstvik | Nairobi, Kenya

Pilgrimage Church of Mary, Queen of Peace | Gottfried Böhm | Neviges, Germany

▸ Paul Goldberger becomes the second architecture critic at the *New York Times*.

▸ Sears Tower in Chicago becomes the world's tallest building.

1974 **Hedmarksmuseet | Sverre Fehn | Hamar, Norway**

Church of Hallgrimur | Guðjón Samúelsson | Reykjavík, Iceland

Foire Internationale de Dakar | Lamoureux, Marin and Bonamy | Fidak, Dakar, Senegal

Gunma Museum of Fine Arts | Arata Isozaki | Takasaki, Japan

Hirshhorn Museum and Sculpture Garden | Skidmore, Owings & Merrill | Washington, DC, United States

Indian Institute of Management | Louis I. Kahn | Ahmedabad, India

▸ Robert Caro's *The Power Broker: Robert Moses and the Fall of New York* published.

1975 Multihalle | Frei Otto | Mannheim, Germany

Art Center College of Design | Craig Ellwood | Pasadena, California, United States

Les Étoiles Housing | Jean Renaudie | Ivry-sur-Seine, France

Walden 7 | Ricardo Bofill | Barcelona, Spain

Willis Faber and Dumas Headquarters | Norman Foster | Ipswich, England

▸ *Architectural Design* publishes a special "Women in Architecture" issue.

▸ The Council of Europe adopts the European Charter of the Architectural Heritage.

1976 Bagsværd Church | Jørn Utzon | Bagsværd, Denmark

La MéMé Medical Faculty Housing | Lucien Kroll | Louvain, Belgium

Oversea-Chinese Banking Corporation Centre | I. M. Pei | Singapore

Royal National Theatre | Denys Lasdun | London, England

Washington Metro | Harry Weese | Washington, DC, United States

▸ MoMA holds the *Architecture of the École des Beaux-Arts* exhibition.

1977 Centre Georges Pompidou | Renzo Piano and Richard Rogers | Paris, France

Science Museum | Sumet Jumsai Associates | Bangkok, Thailand

Yale Center for British Art | Louis I. Kahn | New Haven, Connecticut, United States

▸ Charles Jencks's *The Language of Post-Modern Architecture* published.

▸ Christopher Alexander's *A Pattern Language* published.

1978 Brion-Vega Cemetery | Carlo Scarpa | San Vito d'Altivole, Italy

Danish National Bank | Arne Jacobsen, Hans Dissing, and Otto Weitling | Copenhagen, Denmark

Meritxell Sanctuary | Ricardo Bofill | Canillo, Andorra

Neue Staatsbibliothek Berlin | Hans Scharoun | Berlin, Germany
Sainsbury Centre for Visual Arts | Norman Foster | Norwich, England

East Building, National Gallery of Art | I. M. Pei | Washington, DC, United States

▸ Rem Koolhaas's *Delirious New York* published.

▸ Stanley Tigerman creates *The Titanic* collage of Ludwig Mies van der Rohe's Crown Hall (1956) sinking.

▸ Colin Rowe's *Collage City* published.

1979 The Atheneum | Richard Meier | New Harmony, Indiana, United States

Alexandra Road Housing | Camden Architects Department | London, England

Z Bank | Günther Domenig | Vienna, Austria

▸ Phyllis Lambert founds the Canadian Centre for Architecture in Montreal.

▸ Francis D. K. Ching's *Architecture: Form, Space, and Order* published.

▸ International Building Exhibition (IBA) initiated in Berlin.

▸ Philip Johnson awarded the inaugural Pritzker Architecture Prize.

▸ Philip Johnson appears on the cover of *Time* magazine.

1980 Thorncrown Chapel | E. Fay Jones | Eureka Springs, Arkansas, United States

Crystal Cathedral | Johnson Burgee | Garden Grove, California, United States

Steinkopf Community Centre | Uytenbogaardt & Macaskill | Steinkopf, South Africa

▸ Aldo Rossi designs his floating Teatro del Mondo.

▸ First Venice Architecture Biennale held.

▸ Inaugural year of the Aga Khan Award for Architecture.

▸ Kenneth Frampton's *Modern Architecture: A Critical History* published.

▸ The National Building Museum founded in Washington, DC.

1981 Hajj Terminal | Skidmore, Owings & Merrill | Jeddah, Saudi Arabia

Sangath | Balkrishna Doshi | Ahmeadabad, India

Westin Brisas Hotel Ixtapa | Ricardo Legorreta | Ixtapa, Mexico

▸ Bernard Tschumi's *The Manhattan Transcripts* published.

▸ François Mitterrand begins his *Grands Projets* in Paris.

▸ Team X dissolves.

▸ Tom Wolfe's *From Bauhaus to Our House* published.

1982 SESC Pompéia | Lino Bo Bardi | São Paulo, Brazil

Atlantis Condominium | Arquitectonica | Miami, Florida, United States

Byker Wall Housing | Ralph Erskine | Newcastle upon Tyne, England

Kuwait National Assembly Building | Jørn Utzon | Kuwait City, Kuwait

Museum Abteiberg | Hans Hollein | Mönchengladbach, Germany

Università degli Studi di Urbino "Carlo Bo" | Giancarlo De Carlo | Urbino, Italy

- ▶ *El Croquis* magazine founded in Spain.
- ▶ First version of AutoCAD released.
- ▶ Competition held for the Humana Building in Louisville, Kentucky.
- ▶ Maya Lin's Vietnam Veterans Memorial completed in Washington, DC.
- ▶ Competition held in Paris for Parc de la Villette.

1983 National Assembly Building | Louis I. Kahn | Dhaka, Bangladesh

Kanchanjunga Apartments | Charles Correa | Mumbai, India

Le Palais d'Abraxas Housing | Ricardo Bofill | Paris, France

Portland Building | Michael Graves | Portland, Oregon, United States

San Juan Capistrano Library | Michael Graves | San Juan Capistrano, California, United States

- ▶ Construction begins on Seaside, a New Urbanist town in Florida.

1984 Neue Staatsgalerie | James Stirling Michael Wilford and Associates | Stuttgart, Germany

Cube Houses | Piet Blom | Rotterdam, Netherlands

Dayabumi Complex | BEP, MAA | Kuala Lumpur, Malaysia

Myyrmäki Church | Juha Leiviskä | Vantaa, Finland

San Cataldo Cemetery | Aldo Rossi | Modena, Italy

- ▶ Swiss Architecture Museum (SAM) founded in Basel, Switzerland.

1985 Hongkong and Shanghai Bank Corporation Headquarters | Norman Foster | Hong Kong, China

Humana Building | Michael Graves | Louisville, Kentucky, United States

Middleton Inn | Clark and Menefee | Charleston, South Carolina, United States

Qatar University | Kamal el Kafrawi | Doha, Qatar

Tuwaiq Palace | Frei Otto and Buro Happold | Riyadh, Saudi Arabia

- ▶ Danish Architecture Centre (DAC) founded in Copenhagen.

1986 Museo National de Arte Romano | Rafael Moneo | Mérida, Spain

Lloyd's of London | Richard Rogers | London, England

Lotus Temple | Fariborz Sahba | New Delhi, India

Niamey Grand Market | KPDV | Niamey, Niger

Wisma Dharmala Tower | Paul Rudolph | Jakarta, Indonesia

- ▶ *Detail* magazine founded in Germany.

1987 Institut du Monde Arabe | Jean Nouvel | Paris, France

Centennial Hall | Kazuo Shinohara | Tokyo, Japan

Menil Collection | Renzo Piano | Houston, Texas, United States

- ▶ Peter Greenaway's *The Belly of an Architect* released.

1988 Museo Brasileiro da Escultura | Paulo Mendes da Rocha São Paulo, Brazil

Church on the Water | Tadao Ando | Hokkaido, Japan

Mityana Pilgrims' Centre Shrine | Justus Dahinden | Namugongo, Uganda

Residential Complex with Studio Tower | John Hejduk | Berlin, Germany

Ustrón Sanatorium Complex | PPBO | Ustrón, Poland

- ▶ Álvaro Siza awarded inaugural European Union Prize for Contemporary Architecture|Mies van der Rohe Award.
- ▶ MoMA holds its *Deconstructivist Architecture* exhibition.
- ▶ Docomomo International founded in the Netherlands.
- ▶ Netherlands Architecture Institute (now the New Institute) founded in Rotterdam.

1989 Church of the Light | Tadao Ando | Ibaraki-shi, Osaka, Japan

Grande Arche | Paul Andreu | Paris, France

Saint Benedict Chapel | Peter Zumthor | Zumvitg, Switzerland

Vitra Design Museum | Frank Gehry | Weil am Rhein, Germany

Wexner Center for the Arts | Peter Eisenman | Columbus, Ohio, United States

- ▶ The Berlin Wall comes down.
- ▶ Competition held for Paris's Bibliotheque Nationale de France.
- ▶ I. M. Pei wins the inaugural Praemium Imperiale in architecture.
- ▶ Loma Prieta earthquake strikes San Francisco area.

1990 Stadelhofen Station | Santiago Calatrava | Zürich, Switzerland

Cemetery Igualada | Enric Miralles, Carme Pinós | Barcelona, Spain

Haas House | Hans Hollein | Vienna, Austria

Shonandai Cultural Center | Itsuko Hasegawa | Fujisawa, Japan

- ▶ Americans with Disabilities Act (ADA) enacted in the United States.
- ▶ Anyone Corporation founded in New York City.

1991 Sainsbury Wing, National Gallery | Robert Venturi, Denise Scott Brown and Associates | London, England

Honpukuji Water Temple | Tadao Ando | Hyogo, Japan

Norwegian Glacier Museum | Sverre Fehn | Fjaerland, Norway

Stansted Airport | Norman Foster | London, England

1992 Kunsthal | Office for Metropolitan Architecture | Rotterdam, Netherlands

BCE Place | Santiago Calatrava | Toronto, Canada

Inter-University Center for Astronomy and Astrophysics | Charles Correa | Pune, India

Männistö Church | Juha Leiviskä | Kuopio, Finland

Museo La Congiunta | Peter Märkli | Giornico, Switzerland

- ▶ Euro Disney opens in Paris.
- ▶ Herbert Muschamp becomes the third architecture critic at the *New York Times*.
- ▶ Barcelona hosts the Summer Olympics.

1993 Vitra Fire Station | Zaha Hadid Architects | Weil am Rhein, Germany

American Heritage Center | Antoine Predock | Laramie, Wyoming, United States

Jawahar Kala Kendra | Charles Correa | Jaipur, India

Münster City Library | Bolles+Wilson | Münster, Germany

International Terminal Waterloo | Nicholas Grimshaw | London, England

- ▶ Architekturzentrum Wien (AzW) founded in Vienna.
- ▶ Congress for New Urbanism founded.
- ▶ *Architectural Design* releases its "Folding in Architecture" issue.
- ▶ Samuel Mockbee founds the Rural Studio in Alabama.

1994 Bowali Visitor Centre | Glenn Murcutt and Troppo Architects | Kakadu National Park, Australia

Fondation Cartier | Jean Nouvel | Paris, France

Kansai International Airport | Renzo Piano | Osaka, Japan

Lyon Airport Railway Station | Santiago Calatrava | Lyon, France

- ▶ Channel Tunnel connecting England and France opens.
- ▶ Competition held for the expansion of New York's MoMA.
- ▶ US General Services Administration (GSA) initiates the Design Excellence Program.

1995 Kandalama Hotel | Geoffrey Bawa | Dambulla, Sri Lanka

Amdavad ni Gufa | Stein, Doshi & Bhalla | Ahmedabad, India

Bibliotheque Nationale de France | Dominique Perrault | Paris, France

Naoshima Contemporary Art Museum | Tadao Ando | Naoshima Island, Japan

Neuroscience Institute | Tod Williams Billie Tsien | La Jolla, California, United States

Phoenix Central Library | Will Bruder | Phoenix, Arizona, United States

- ▶ Competition for Yokohama International Passenger Terminal held.
- ▶ MoMA holds its *Light Construction* exhibition.
- ▶ Rem Koolhaas's *S,M,L,XL* published.

1996 Therme Vals | Peter Zumthor | Vals, Switzerland

Chapel of Santa Maria degli Angeli | Mario Botta | Monte Tamaro, Switzerland

Eastgate Centre | Pearce Partnership | Harare, Zimbabwe

Museu de Arte Contemporânea de Niterói | Oscar Niemeyer | Niterói, Brazil

Tokyo International Forum | Rafael Viñoly | Tokyo, Japan

- ▶ Passivhaus Institut founded in Germany.
- ▶ Royal Institute of British Architects (RIBA) holds inaugural Stirling Prize.
- ▶ The Skyscraper Museum founded in New York City.

1997 Guggenheim Museum Bilbao | Frank Gehry | Bilbao, Spain

Chapel of St. Ignatius | Steven Holl | Seattle, Washington, United States

Delft Polytechnic Library | Mecanoo | Delft, Netherlands

Fondation Beyeler | Renzo Piano | Riehen, Switzerland

Getty Center | Richard Meier | Los Angeles, California, United States

Kunsthaus Bregenz | Peter Zumthor | Bregenz, Austria

- ▶ Earthquake hits the Umbria and Marche regions of Italy.
- ▶ Neil Leach's *Rethinking Architecture* published.

1998 Tjibaou Cultural Centre | Renzo Piano Building Workshop | Nouméa, New Caledonia

B 018 | Bernard Khoury | Beirut, Lebanon

Kiasma Museum of Contemporary Art | Steven Holl | Helsinki, Finland

Minnaert Building | Neutelings Riedijk | Utrecht, Netherlands

Portuguese National Pavilion | Álvaro Siza | Lisbon, Portugal

- ▶ Expo 98 held in Lisbon, Portugal.
- ▶ MoMA PS1 Young Architects Program starts in New York City.
- ▶ Number of visitors to Guggenheim Bilbao in its first year reaches 1.36 million.

1999 Jewish Museum Berlin | Daniel Libeskind | Berlin, Germany

Embassies of the Nordic Countries | Berger + Parkkinen, et al. | Berlin, Germany

Fukuoka Prefectural International Hall | Emilio Ambasz | Fukuoka, Japan

Kursaal Auditorium | Rafael Moneo | Donostia-San Sebastián, Spain

Velodrome and Olympic Swimming Pool | Dominique Perrault | Berlin, Germany

- ▶ Architecture for Humanity established.

2000 **Sendai Mediatheque | Toyo Ito | Sendai, Japan**

Cultural and Congress Centre (KKL) | Jean Nouvel | Lucerne, Switzerland

Great Court at the British Museum | Norman Foster | London, England

Museum of Ando Hiroshige | Kengo Kuma | Nakagawa, Japan

Rose Center for Earth and Space | Polshek Partnership | New York City, United States

Waldspirale | Friedensreich Hundertwasser | Darmstadt, Germany

▶ Expo 2000 held in Hannover, Germany.

▶ Inaugural Serpentine Gallery Pavilion in London designed by Zaha Hadid.

▶ Leadership in Energy and Environmental Design (LEED) certification system unveiled.

▶ Millennium festivities held in London.

2001 **Eden Project | Nicholas Grimshaw | Cornwall, England**

Biosphere and Flower Pavilion | Barkow Leibinger | Potsdam, Germany

Quadracci Pavilion | Santiago Calatrava | Milwaukee, Wisconsin, United States

Rouen Concert Hall and Exhibition Complex | Bernard Tschumi | Rouen, France

Virgilio Barco Library | Rogelio Salmona | Bogotá, Colombia

▶ Replica of Villa Savoye (1931) built at National Museum of Australia.

▶ September 11 terrorist attacks destroy the Twin Towers in New York.

2002 **Bibliotheca Alexandrina | Snøhetta | Alexandria, Egypt**

Austrian Cultural Forum | Raimund Abraham | New York City, United States

Cathedral of Our Lady of the Angels | Rafael Moneo | Los Angeles, California, United States

Vulcania | Hans Hollein | Saint-Ours-les-Roches, France

Yokohama International Passenger Terminal | FOA | Yokohama, Japan

▶ Competition held for the National Stadium in Beijing.

▶ Competition held for World Trade Center master plan.

▶ Expo.02 held in Switzerland.

▶ First Solar Decathlon held in Washington, DC.

2003 **Selfridges | Future Systems | Birmingham, England**

Federation Square | LAB Architecture | Melbourne, Australia

Prada Aoyama | Herzog & de Meuron | Tokyo, Japan

Rosenthal Center for Contemporary Art | Zaha Hadid | Cincinnati, Ohio, United States

Walt Disney Concert Hall | Frank Gehry | Los Angeles, California, United States

▶ Daniel Libeskind wins World Trade Center master plan competition.

▶ Nathaniel Kahn's *My Architect* released.

2004 **The Scottish Parliament | Enric Miralles and Benedetta Tagliabue | Edinburgh, Scotland**

21st Century Museum of Contemporary Art | SANAA | Kanazawa, Japan

Casa Das Mudas | Paulo David | Calheta, Portugal

Sharp Centre for Design | Will Alsop | Toronto, Canada

Utrecht University Library | Wiel Arets | Utrecht, Netherlands

▶ Nicolai Ouroussoff becomes the fourth architecture critic at the *New York Times*.

▶ Taipei 101 in Taiwan becomes the world's tallest building.

▶ Zaha Hadid is the first woman awarded the Pritzker Architecture Prize.

2005 **de Young Museum | Herzog & de Meuron | San Francisco, California, United States**

Casa da Música | OMA | Porto, Portugal

Holocaust History Museum, Yad Vashem | Moshe Safdie | Jerusalem, Israel

Santa Caterina Market | EMBT | Barcelona, Spain

Terminal 4, Barajas Airport | Richard Rogers | Madrid, Spain

▶ Peter Eisenman's Memorial to the Murdered Jews of Europe opens in Berlin.

▶ Shenzhen Bi-city Biennale of Urbanism|Architecture founded in China.

2006 **Glass Pavilion, Toledo Museum of Art | SANAA | Toledo, Ohio, United States**

Dutch Embassy | Dick van Gameren and Bjarne Mastenbroek | Addis Ababa, Ethiopia

Institute of Contemporary Art | Diller Scofidio + Renfro | Boston, Massachusetts, United States

Torre Cube | Carme Pinós | Guadalajara, Mexico

Tschuggen Bergoase Wellness Center | Mario Botta | Arosa, Switzerland

▶ MoMA holds its *On-Site: New Architecture in Spain* exhibition.

2007 **Bloch Building, Nelson-Atkins Museum of Art | Steven Holl Architects | Kansas City, Missouri, United States**

España Library | Giancarlo Mazzanti | Santo Domingo, Colombia

Kolumba Museum | Peter Zumthor | Cologne, Germany

Tama Art University Library | Toyo Ito | Tokyo, Japan

Vasconcelos Library | Alberto Kalach | Mexico City, Mexico

2008 Fundação Iberê Camargo | Álvaro Siza | Porto Alegre, Brazil

Ewha Woman's University | Dominique Perrault | Seoul, South Korea

National Stadium | Herzog & de Meuron | Beijing, China

Ningbo History Museum | Amateur Architecture Studio | Ningbo, China

Oslo Opera House | Snøhetta | Oslo, Norway

▶ Inaugural World Architecture Festival held in Barcelona.

▶ Beijing hosts the Summer Olympics.

▶ World Monuments Fund|Knoll Modernism Prize launches.

▶ World urban population exceeds 50 percent for the first time in history.

2009 Aqua Tower | Studio Gang Architects | Chicago, Illinois, United States

Acropolis Museum | Bernard Tschumi | Athens, Greece

Knut Hamsun Centre | Steven Holl Architects | Hamarøy, Norway

Linked Hybrid | Steven Holl Architects | Beijing, China

Termas Geométricas | Germán del Sol | Villarrica, Chile

▶ First phase of the High Line elevated park opens in New York.

2010 MAXXI | Zaha Hadid Architects | Rome, Italy

Musashino Art University Library | Sou Fujimoto | Tokyo, Japan

Rolex Learning Center | SANAA | Lausanne, Switzerland

Tel Aviv Museum of Art | Preston Scott Cohen | Tel Aviv, Israel

Yas Viceroy Hotel | Asymptote | Abu Dhabi, United Arab Emirates

▶ Burj Khalifa in Dubai becomes the world's tallest building.

2011 Metropol Parasol | J. Mayer H. | Seville, Spain

Clyfford Still Museum | Allied Works | Denver, Colorado, United States

Liyuan Library | Li Xiaodong | Jiaojiehe, China

Mapungubwe Interpretation Centre | Peter Rich Architects | Johannesburg, South Africa

Museo Soumaya | Fernando Romero | Mexico City, Mexico

▶ Michael Kimmelman becomes the fifth architecture critic at the *New York Times*.

▶ Earthquake and tsunami strike off the coast of Japan.

2012 CCTV Headquarters | Office for Metropolitan Architecture | Beijing, China

Antinori Winery | Archea Associati | Bargino, Italy

Barnes Foundation | Tod Williams Billie Tsien | Philadelphia, Pennsylvania, United States

Book Mountain | MVRDV | Spijkenisse, Netherlands

Heydar Aliyev Centre | Zaha Hadid Architects | Baku, Azerbaijan

RMIT Design Hub | Sean Godsell | Melbourne, Australia

▶ London hosts the Summer Olympics.

▶ Lower Manattan loses power when Superstorm Sandy hits the northeastern United States.

2013 Xiangshan Campus, China Academy of Art | Amateur Architecture Studio | Hangzhou, China

Cardboard Cathedral | Shigeru Ban | Christchurch, New Zealand

Danish Maritime Museum | Bjarke Ingels Group | Helsingør, Denmark

Fogo Island Inn | Saunders Architecture | Fogo, Canada

Sancaklar Mosque | Emre Arolat Architects | Istanbul, Turkey

Shenzhen Bao'an International Airport | Fuksas | Shenzhen, China

▶ Denise Scott Brown says she is owed a "Pritzker Prize inclusion ceremony."

▶ MoMA announces plans to demolish the neighboring American Folk Art Museum.

▶ Museum for Architectural Drawing founded in Berlin.

2014 Markthal | MVRDV | Rotterdam, Netherlands

Aspen Art Museum | Shigeru Ban | Aspen, Colorado, United States

Clark Art Institute | Tadao Ando | Williamstown, Massachusetts, United States

National Library of Latvia | Gunnar Birkerts | Riga, Latvia

Philharmonic Hall | Barozzi Veiga | Szczecin, Poland

▶ Mies Crown Hall Americas Prize launches.

▶ Competition held for the Nobel Center in Stockholm.

▶ Valencia sues Santiago Calatrava over City of Arts and Sciences.

▶ Vandals damage painted glass in Notre Dame du Haut (1955).

2015 The Broad | Diller Scofidio + Renfro | Los Angeles, California, United States

Grace Farms River Building | SANAA | New Canaan, Connecticut, United States

Nanyang Technological University Learning Hub | Heatherwick Studio | Singapore

Shanghai Tower | Gensler | Shanghai, China

Taichung Metropolitan Opera House | Toyo Ito | Taichung, Taiwan

▶ Guggenheim Helsinki competition held.

▶ Inaugural Chicago Architecture Biennial takes place.

▶ Willis Tower (née Sears Tower) in Chicago sells for $1.3 billion.

▶ Japan drops Zaha Hadid Architects as the designer of its New National Stadium.

GENERAL BIBLIOGRAPHY

For a complete bibliography visit archidose.blogspot.com /p/100-years-100-buildings.html

20th-Century World Architecture. London: Phaidon, 2012.

Baker, Geoffrey H. *Le Corbusier: An Analysis of Form*. 3rd ed. London: Spon Press, 1996

Banham, Reyner. *Age of the Masters: A Personal View of Modern Architecture*. New York: Harper & Row, 1975.

Botey, Josep Ma. *Oscar Niemeyer: Works and Projects*. Barcelona: Gustavo Gili, 1996.

Brownlee, David B., and David G. De Long. *Louis I. Kahn: In the Realm of Architecture*. New York: Rizzoli, 1991.

Carranza, Luis E. and Fernando Luiz Lara. *Modern Architecture in Latin America: Art, Technology, and Utopia*. Austin: University of Texas Press, 2014.

Carter, Peter. *Mies van der Rohe at Work*. London: Phaidon, 1999.

Cohen, Jean-Louis. *The Future of Architecture Since 1889*. London: Phaidon, 2012.

——, ed. *Le Corbusier: An Atlas of Modern Landscapes*. New York: The Museum of Modern Art, 2013.

Cook, John W. and Heinrich Klotz, eds. *Conversations with Architects*. New York: Praeger, 1973.

Damaz, Paul F. *Art in Latin American Architecture*. New York: Reinhold, 1963.

Fernández-Galiano, Luis. *Atlas: Global Architecture circa 2000*. Bilbao: Fundación BBVA, 2007.

Fleig, Karl. *Alvar Aalto*. London: Thames and Hudson, 1975.

Fondation Le Corbusier. www.fondationlecorbusier.fr

Frampton, Kenneth. *The Evolution of 20th Century Architecture: A Synoptic Account*. Vienna: Springer, 2007.

——. *Le Corbusier: Architect of the Twentieth Century*. New York: Harry N. Abrams, 2002.

Frampton, Kenneth et al., eds. *World Architecture 1900–2000: A Critical Mosaic*, 10 vols. Beijing: China Architecture & Building Press, 2000.

Gans, Deborah. *The Le Corbusier Guide*. New York: Princeton Architectural Press, 1987.

Glancey, Jonathan. *Modern World Architecture: Classic Buildings of Our Time*. London: Carlton Books, 2011.

Gregory, Rob. *Key Contemporary Buildings: Plans, Sections and Elevations*. New York: W. W. Norton, 2008.

Heyer, Paul. *Architects on Architecture: New Directions in America, New and Enlarged Edition*. New York: Walker, 1978.

Ibelings, Hans. *European Architecture Since 1890*. Amsterdam: Sun, 2011.

Jordy, William H. *American Buildings and Their Architects, Volume 5: The Impact of European Modernism in the Mid-Twentieth Century*. Oxford: Oxford University Press, 1986.

Kimmel, Laurence, Bruno Santa Cecília, and Anke Tiggemann. *Architectural Guide: Brazil*. Berlin: DOM, 2013.

Lobell, John. *Between Silence and Light: Spirit in the Architecture of Louis I. Kahn*. Boston: Shambhala, 1985.

Mertins, Detlef. *Mies*. New York: Phaidon, 2014.

Murray, Scott. *Contemporary Curtain Wall Architecture*. New York: Princeton Architectural Press, 2009.

Pfeiffer, Bruce Brooks. *Frank Lloyd Wright: The Masterworks*. New York: Rizzoli, 1993.

The Phaidon Atlas of Contemporary World Architecture. London: Phaidon, 2004.

The Phaidon Atlas of 21st Century World Architecture. London: Phaidon, 2008.

Puglisi, Luigi Prestinenza. *New Directions in Contemporary Architecture: Evolutions and Revolutions in Building Design Since 1988*. Chichester, UK: John Wiley & Sons, 2008.

Quantrill, Malcolm. *Alvar Aalto: A Critical Study*. New York: New Amsterdam Books, 1989.

Self, Ronnie. *The Architecture of Art Museums: A Decade of Design: 2000–2010*. London: Routledge, 2014.

Schulze, Franz, and Edward Windhorst. *Mies van der Rohe: A Critical Biography, New and Revised Edition*. Chicago: University of Chicago Press, 2014.

Sharp, Dennis. *Twentieth Century Architecture: A Visual History*. New York: Facts on File, 1991.

Smith, G. E. Kidder. *Source Book of American Architecture: 500 Notable Buildings from the 10th Century to the Present*. New York: Princeton Architectural Press, 1996.

Sudjic, Deyan. *Fifty Modern Buildings That Changed the World*. London: Conran Octopus, 2015.

Tietz, Jürgen. *The Story of Architecture of the 20th Century*. Cologne: Könemann, 1999.

Twentieth Century Society. *100 Buildings 100 Years*. London: Batsford, 2015.

Weston, Richard. *Alvar Aalto*. London: Phaidon, 1997.

——. *Architecture Visionaries*. London: Laurence King, 2015.

ACKNOWLEDGMENTS

This book would not have happened if Amy Barkow had not put me in touch with Holly La Due at Prestel. So thanks goes first and foremost to Amy for the recommendation and to Holly for guiding me through the process and making the book so much better than otherwise.

No architecture book is complete without some appealing photographs to make the words go down that much easier. So thanks then to Jordan Pace and Jane Robbins Mize for their hard work in the frustrating task of finding photographs and obtaining permissions; thanks to Sophia Gibb at VIEW for helping with my numerous repeated requests; thanks

to the architects and institutions—too numerous to list here—that supplied me with photos of their buildings; and thanks to the photographers I'm indebted to for their generosity: Ximo Michavila, Trevor Patt, Klaas Vermaas, Pedro Kok, Jens Kristian Seier, Darren Bradley, Flavio Bragaia, Bryan Boyer, Ken McCown, Marcelo Donadussi, and Nathan Umstead.

And lastly, thanks to my wife, Karen, and my daughter, Clare, for putting up with my lack of free time on yet another book.

PHOTOGRAPHY CREDITS

© ADCK – Centre Culturel Tjibaou/RPBW/Ph. John Gollings: 177; Richard Anderson: 103; Rainer Arlt / Leibniz Institute for Astrophysics Potsdam: 23; Iwan Baan: 205, 211; Hassan Bagheri: 107(b); Luc Boegly/Artedia: 37(b); Luc Boegly/Artedia / VIEW: 167; Francesco Bolis Courtesy Fondazione MAXXI: 201; Bryan Boyer: 73; Darren Bradley: 43, 109; Flavio Bragaia: 67, 121(t); Bitter Bredt: 179(t); © Richard Brine/VIEW/ARTHUR IMAGES: 49; James Brittain: 115; Rene Burri / Magnum Photos / Agentur Focus: 77; Stefan Buzas © CISA A. Palladio, Vicenza: 137; David Cardelús: 15; Carol M. Highsmith Archive, Library of Congress, Prints and Photographs Division: 55, 57, 79, 83; Centraal Museum, Utrecht / Ernst Moritz: 29(b); Centraal Museum, Utrecht / Ernst Moritz / Pictoright: 29(t); © Collection Artedia / VIEW: 69, 97, 185; Randall Connaughton: 141; Stephane Couturier/Artedia / VIEW: 155; © Edward Denison, 2015: 207(t); Marcelo Donadussi: 101; Ralf Ganter, courtesy of Foundation Haus Schminke: 47; Leonardo Finotti / photo@leonardofinotti.com: 87; Arnout Fonck: 107(t); Fondazione Renzo Piano: 135; © Dennis Gilbert / VIEW: 13, 181, 189; John Gollings: 169; © Fernando Guerra / VIEW: 4–5, 197; © Roland Halbe/ARTUR IMAGES: 113; Steve Hall © Hedrich Blessing: 199; Brian Hazell: 57; Lv Hengzhong/Amateur Architecture Studio: 207(b); John Hill: 37(t), 80, 139, 161, 173(b); Perry Hooper © Grimshaw: 183(t); Naquib Hossain: 147; Daniel Hundven-Clements / VIEW: 105; Courtesy of Illinois Institute of Technology: 93; Courtesy of Indianapolis Museum of Art: 95; Jan Haug – Domkirkeoddens photoarcive: 129; Xavier de Jauréguiberry: 27; Neil Keogh © Grimshaw:

183(b); Pedro Kok: 73, 145; Nelson Kon: 157; © Kunsthal Rotterdam, Jeroen Musch: 165; Ian Lambot: 151; © Jay Langlois | Owens-Corning: 143; Robert LaPrelle, © 2013 Kimbell Art Museum: 125; David Leventi / Courtesy Rick Wester Fine Art: 117; Loews Philadelphia Hotel: 45; © Thomas Mayer/ARTUR IMAGES: 91(t); Ken McCrown: 19, 61; © MAK center / Photo by Joshua White: 25(b); Ximo Michavila: 35(r), 39, 127, 153, 175(b); Museum Het Schip: 21; Trevor Patt: 25(t), 91(b), 173(t), 193; Courtesy of Phillips Exeter Academy; photo credit: Brian F. Crowley: 123; Provast @ Ossip van Duijvebode: 209; Fabián Pulti: 71; © Tomas Riehle/ARTUR IMAGES: 31; © Paolo Rosselli/ARTUR IMAGES: 59; Sergio Ruiz: 17; © Andy Ryan: 6–7, 195; Image courtesy SACYR, photograph Fernando Alda: 203; Courtesy of Salk Institute: 2–3, 111; Nicolás Saieh: 85; Dominic Sansoni/ThreeBlindMen: 171; © Robert Schezen/Esto: 63; Guenter Schneider: 179(b); © Jörg Schöner/ARTUR IMAGES: 121(b); seier+seier: 35(l), 133; Luca Senise: 119(t); Filippo Simonetti: 53; Timothy Soar, courtesy of Venturi, Scott Brown and Associates, Inc.: 163(b); The Solomon R. Guggenheim Museum, New York. Photograph: David Heald © SRGF, NY: 99; Fernando Stankuns: 119(b); Nathan Umstead: 65; Klaas Vermaas: 33; Shinichi Waki: 159; Matt Wargo, courtesy of Venturi, Scott Brown and Associates, Inc.: 163(t); Anthony Weller / VIEW: 175(t); © Nathan Willock / VIEW: 89, 187; Klaas Vermaas: 149; De Young Museum © Fine Arts Museums of San Francisco: 191(t); De Young Museum, Fern Court © Fine Arts Museums of San Francisco: 191(b); © David Zidlicky 41.